God on Life

'Is life worth living? Is it worth it? Who killed "a meaningless life"? Through stories, brilliant observations and personal reflections Paul takes us on a journey with King Solomon to reflect on these crucial questions about life.

I found the book insightful, thought-provoking and encouraging.'

Bev Thomas, Spring Harvest speaker, Evangelical Alliance Council

'In this book, Paul addresses the futility of life without God and that as spiritual beings we can never be fully satisfied with anything material that we acquire in our brief human existence. Only by knowing our creator and living in a right relationship with him, can we ever experience a truly meaningful life and the eternal hope it brings us. This book will be a great help to individuals who are on a journey to faith. It will also serve as a spiritual "health-check" to those of us who have been Christians for some time.'

Noel Richards, singer and songwriter

'Paul Griffiths covers his subject well, comparing Ecclesiastes to the present day. It is a good read especially if you are searching for meaning to life in a meaningless age.'

Ian Leitch, The Heralds Trust

God on Life

PAUL GRIFFITHS

Authentic
LIFESTYLE

Published 2003 by Paternoster Press

09 08 07 06 05 04 03   7 6 5 4 3 2 1

Authentic Lifestyle is an imprint of Authentic Media,
PO Box 300, Carlisle, Cumbria CA3 0QS, UK
and PO Box 1047, Waynesboro, GA 30830–2047, USA
www.paternoster-publishing.com

British Library Cataloguing in Publication Data
A catalogue record for this book is available from the British Library

ISBN 1–85078–547–3

Typeset by Waverley Typesetters, Galashiels
Print Management by Adare Carwin
Printed and Bound in Denmark by Nørhaven Paperback

Contents

This book is dedicated to:

Nick Baldwin, Martin Bell, Bill Hewis, Andrew James,
Steve Jenkins, Sharon Lanfear and Steve Taylor

'Enablers in the ADVENTURE'

Foreword

Paul Griffiths is a gifted evangelist. Like many who have such a gift, Paul is able to make friends easily, come to know the hearts of people and communicate with them on their terms. He is also a wonderful storyteller.

I suspect that Ecclesiastes is one of the lesser known books of the Bible. Its meaning and relevance to contemporary life does not always jump out at us. Paul has the ability to bring the storyteller's eye to Scripture and make the connections so that the profound wisdom of Ecclesiastes rises to the surface. The title *God on Life* describes very well Paul's ability to release the power of Holy Scripture.

MARTIN ROBINSON
National Director of Together in Mission

Introduction

When I was in my teens I made a decision that would influence my life.

It is fair to say that at the time I did not fully understand the significance of that decision or experience even partially the consequences of it. And yet, as I glance back, the potential for something different was established because of what occurred on that Thursday afternoon at a Llanmadoc campsite on the Gower Peninsular.

What happened? Well, very simply, I was introduced to an old book, which I decided to read. Over the years this book has proved to be a constant source of guidance and help. I've worn out several copies of it and it looks like the latest one is about to fall apart.

I love the adventure of life. This book has enabled me, even dared me, to enjoy life's journey.

Don't misunderstand me, I'm not saying that my life has not had its fill of ups and downs. A friend of mine once described life as like an assault course – but what potential for adventure and survival! This book was given to make us aware of a deeper, almost invisible to the human eye, take on it all.

On reading this book I discovered that within it there were a number of smaller books, one of which is called Ecclesiastes. *God on Life* is all about this smaller book and how I think it relates to life today. Ecclesiastes was written to give us wisdom for life.

It was probably about ten years ago that I began to look seriously at what this smaller book of Ecclesiastes is all about. I had read it before, but never given it any thought, but then I read something that somebody had written about it and I was hooked.

Lots of people have contributed to my book, some un-knowingly. To all I express my thankfulness. A particular note of appreciation goes to the many gatherings of people who have allowed me to talk to them about what I have discovered about life from Ecclesiastes. Also, thanks go to Paternoster for publishing my book, Peter and Jean Walker for editing the original text, and then Jill Morris for adding the finishing touches and making it presentable.

There is something sacred about life, in the midst of daily reports of the evil that some humans enact, within the routine of daily existence and living, against the backdrop of human fragility. Deep within, many know that life is far more unique and inspiring than we presently experience.

The book of Ecclesiastes and my book about this ancient guide to life attempt to lead us to that sacred place.

Chapter 1

God on … is life worth living?

Is life worth living? Is it?

That's the question on the mind of a friend of mine right now. Her husband left her a couple of weeks ago because he is in love with another woman. There she is, struggling to make ends meet, with the prospect of having to bring up their children on her own, rejected and with no sure way forward. Is life worth living? Is it?

Another friend called Brian was also asking this question recently. For thirty years he has worked for a company, given it the best years of his life. More often than not he has put the company before his family. Holidays have been cut short or not taken. Working days have been far longer than they should have been. Special family days, like birthdays or anniversaries, have been sacrificed for the company. And what's happened? A merger, with the new company viewing him as surplus to requirements. Thirty years to get where he's got to. A life's work, and now he's surplus to requirements. Is life worth living? Is it?

But, you know, it's not just my friends who are asking this question. I read in the newspaper about a fellow who's also asking it. I'm sure we can all understand why. He goes to work in the morning with a wife and two sons, comes home in the evening to find out that he has only one son left. That afternoon, while crossing the road, one son is knocked down and killed. His wife, who hears the accident from their nearby house, goes to investigate and is killed by another car on the same road. What's the point? All that love, all that time, all that commitment, and what's left? Only memories! Sure, great memories, but only memories. Is life worth living? Is it?

And what about the person who was lucky enough to win the British lottery? There she is on the Saturday night with her partner, celebrating the fact that she has become a millionairess, only to find in the following weeks that her world falls apart as she and her partner fight over whose money it actually is and what should be done with it. The lottery told her, 'It could be you!' It was. The question she wants answered is, was it worth it?

What's the point? Is it worth it? Is life worth living? These are some of the heart-wrenching questions that are born often in the depths of despair.

These questions are not new. Philosophers have been discussing them for centuries. Plato, Aristotle and, more recently, Jean-Paul Sartre and Friedrich Nietzsche have all tried to answer these fundamental questions of life.

Is life worth living? It's a question that has probably never been asked on any quiz show, yet it should have been, for many of the contestants who have appeared on such shows will have tried at some point in their lives to answer it.

This question is the focus of Solomon in the first chapter of his journal, though in Solomon's case he asked this question not from feelings of depression or tragedy but rather because, although he had all the things that life can offer, he still felt as if something was missing.

Please note that this is no diary of a man in mid-life crisis, a lecturer who out of boredom and an awareness that life is passing him by decides to embark on a foolish infatuation with one of his students. Solomon isn't at the male menopause. These are not the writings of a pessimist on a downer.

Solomon is, as I have hinted already, a man who is all there. In fact, very rarely in the history of the world have there been people privileged to live as Solomon did. He was a king, a king of Israel, a man of great wealth who lacked nothing that his world could give him. His are the writings of a Mr Successful.

In the opening chapter of Ecclesiastes (Ecclesiastes means 'the preacher' or 'the teacher': see the opening few words of the book) Solomon tells us of a quest that he has gone on. Like the quests of many of the explorers of the past, Solomon's was a quest to find that which he had an inkling about, but at the time no evidence.

His quest? To find the answer to one of the most fundamental questions of life: 'Is life worth living?' Or, to use a modern-day phrase, 'When the fat lady sang, was it worth it?'

Within this chapter I want to look at what Solomon writes about his journey: about how he took it, about what occurred, about his findings and about the conclusions that he drew from it. You will find that it is a fascinating journey.

Before we look at what Solomon says to us in regard to 'Is life worth living?' I want to make several comments about the biblical book of Ecclesiastes. These are important points to note, for they will be the basis of all that will follow in this book.

Firstly, what we have in Ecclesiastes is Solomon's journal, a diary. It records the activities and thoughts of the man as he travels through uncharted waters. It would be comparable to Stanley's diaries of his exploring of Africa. It's an exciting, must-be-read sort of book.

Secondly, with regard to the biblical category that the book belongs to, we would refer to it as wisdom literature. Solomon was one of the wisest men who ever lived, and what we have here are his wise comments and observations on life.

Thirdly, in contradiction to the normal flow of books, Ecclesiastes is unusual in that the conclusion to the book comes at the beginning and not at the end. So keen is Solomon to share his insights with people that he leaves no time after introducing himself to make us aware of his findings. One might add that his wisdom is evident in the fact that he obviously knew how to sell a book. We have on the front cover a sensational, provocative statement about life:

> 'Meaningless! Meaningless!'
> says the Teacher.
> 'Utterly meaningless!
> Everything is meaningless.'

Fourthly, although it is an old book, what you and I will become aware of as we move through Solomon's experiences is that there is a spooky, contemporary feel to Ecclesiastes.

OK then, so what does Solomon have to say to us about his journey into the question of life?

Solomon's qualifications for speaking and being listened to

Every year in the US Congress the President makes a televised speech, the State of the Union Address, informing the House and the American people on the state of the Nation. When analysing the way in which this speech is received, television critics often observe how this has very little to do with its content or style of delivery, or indeed the actual state of the nation. Rather, it has to do with the perceived calibre of the man who is making it.

If the speaker is viewed as trustworthy, then the speech will be well received; if the speaker is regarded as being of questionable character, then the speech is sure to be dismissed. On more than one occasion the American press have commented on how people prefer to watch television or videos rather than listen to someone whose integrity is in doubt.

Solomon knew that to be heard you not only have to have something to say but also the qualifications to say it. Therefore one of the first things that we find Solomon doing in his opening chapter is pointing out to us his qualifications.

He says that in regard to his findings about the answer to the question of life we need to be aware that he committed himself to this search – he was devoted. He gave time, money and energy; he resolved himself to discover the answer. His conclusions are not ad hoc thoughts. His quest is not his hobby on the side. These are the findings he has made after giving himself to the task of answering the question. His is the commitment of the Olympian. And, by the way, do note that he was well able to carry out a great search:

*I was king over Israel ... grown and increased in wisdom
more than anyone ... before me ...*

Solomon tells us that he devoted himself to study. He
researched his subject. The original Hebrew word translated
here as 'devoted' carried with it the idea of researching to
the root. Solomon's study wasn't a superficial, simple
external examination: he went for X-rays and internal
investigation. He gave the subject a thorough examination.
He rolled up his sleeves and dug for gold in the libraries.
The academic searching that Solomon carried out here is
what we would expect of a PhD student.

But more than just studying his subject, what Solomon
also tells us is that he explored it. To explore means to
experience. He didn't just read about the joy of sex – he
went and experienced it. He didn't just talk to people who
were in the pop business, or architecture, agriculture or
horticulture – he went and got stuck in himself.

So deep was his devotion to studying and exploring
thoroughly his topic that he could say at the end of his
investigations that he had studied and explored all things.
'I have', says Solomon, 'fulfilled all my fantasies. I have
fulfilled all your fantasies. I have done the "what if".
What if I have an affair? What if I have a new car? What
if I get a new job? What if I had got that degree? What if
we get that house? What if I win the lottery? Whatever
the "what ifs", I have realised them; I have left no stone
unturned.'

Now, in regard to the sphere of his search, we need to
note that he does put one restriction on it. According to
Solomon, there are two ways of looking at life – two frames
within which we can hang it. One can look at life 'under
heaven' or 'under the sun'. These two perspectives are
poles apart, as much so as were the opinions in Columbus's

day of those who believed that the world was flat and those who were sure it was round.

To live 'under heaven' is to live within a framework that incorporates the existence of God. So life is not three score years and ten and then nothing, but three score years and ten and then eternity. The parameters stretch further than birth and death. To live under heaven is to believe in a spiritual dimension to life as well as a physical one; a spiritual dimension that the Judeo-Christian God inhabits.

An alternative way of looking at life is from 'under the sun'. This is to view life without the existence of and/or worship of the Almighty God. This does not mean that you do not believe in a spiritual side to life or in the existence of God. Rather it is a view wherein the Christian God, or, as he would have been in Solomon's day, the Jewish God, is not held in first place. So this description of living life under the sun can be used to define an atheist or a spiritually orientated person.

Now, what Solomon does within his book is initially to set sail within the framework of life 'under the sun', without the existence of the Bible's God. He enquires if, within this context, the answer to the question 'Is life worth living?' is to be found. Is he going to fall off the end of the world, or what?

Occasionally, as we have seen, there might have been questions of confidence about the speaker of the State of the Union Address. But Solomon leaves us in no doubt. He is qualified to speak and warrants our attention.

Solomon's discovery

One of the most remarkable stories of the twentieth century was that of a lady by the name of Rose Kennedy. In many senses Rose Kennedy lived the life of the fortunate few. When her husband died in the 1960s she was left $350 million. Her clan was characterised by power, wealth and glamour. She herself was an incredible woman, the daughter of a congressman, wife of an ambassador, mother of a president, the only woman ever to send three sons to the American Senate.

What is interesting about Rose's life is that alongside the wealth and prestige she also had to face an unfairly high amount of personal tragedy both in her family life and personal life.

In a recent newspaper article I discovered some of Rose Kennedy's thoughts about her life. As someone who had experienced the scenarios of prestige and pain, her comments are quite enlightening:

> *Life has squeezed the joy out of my existence.*

> *Life becomes primarily an act of the will,*
> *doing what is necessary to keep you going.*

> *Some people say that time heals all wounds, I don't agree, the*
> *wounds remain.*

What Solomon says, albeit many centuries earlier, is that his findings are the same as Rose's. Life sucks. At the end of the day there is only deflation, depression, disillusionment.

> *'Meaningless! Meaningless!' [repeated for emphasis]*
> *says the teacher.*
> *'Utterly meaningless!*
> *Everything is meaningless.'*

Life, says Solomon, is like the potential you see in a sports person who promises so much – the world is his or her oyster – but who for some reason doesn't fully deliver, and rather mockingly hangs around always suggesting what could have been.

Solomon's findings are the same as those of Jean-Paul Sartre: 'the disconcerting truth is that we cannot find happiness in anything created or human'. This is true whether we search for it in the Hollywood life or the mundane life of a rural backwater town.

A while back, one of the big films was *Doc Hollywood*, starring Michael J. Fox. On the way to an interview in Hollywood, this newly qualified doctor has a car accident and a subsequent run-in with the law, which sees him doing community service in a backwater town. What the film does is portray the difficult decision that the doctor has to make as he comes to see that true life is found in this backwater town and not in the glitz of Hollywood. It is here that he will find love and here that his dreams are waiting to be fulfilled. The film rewrites and presents a new understanding of the American dream.

What Solomon does is cast doubt on whether either the backwater town or the glitz of Hollywood actually offers a life worth living. In fact, says Solomon, both lives are meaningless.

Solomon's reasoning is, when all is said and done, what has life given us? What was in it for us that lasts? When you are on your deathbed, what will be your legacy?

What does man gain from all his labour at which he toils under the sun?

Can you not see our futility in the cycle of life? We make no difference; we are here but for a season:

Generations come and generations go, but the earth remains for ever.

If we had looked we would have seen such futility in creation:

> *The sun rises and the sun sets, and hurries back to*
> *where it rises.*
> *The wind blows to the south and turns to the north;*
> *round and round it goes, ever returning on its course.*
> *All streams flow into the sea, yet the sea is never full.*
> *To the place the streams come from, there they return again.*

Look at our appetites for knowledge:

> *The eye never has enough of seeing, nor the ear its fill of*
> *hearing.*

There is nothing new to discover. What is more, new inventions are only the application of old principles or the discovery of what has always been:

> *What has been will be again, what has been done*
> *will be done again;*
> *there is nothing new under the sun.*
> *Is there anything of which one can say, 'Look! This is*
> *something new'?*
> *It was here already, long ago; it was here before our time.*

See, there is not even any lasting fame, no remembrance. Our names are, as Keats says, 'writ in water'.

> *There is no remembrance of men of old,*
> *and even those who are yet to come*
> *will not be remembered by those who follow.*

What Solomon is saying, again and again, is that under the sun there is nothing that can fulfil our quest. Futility abounds. It could have been Solomon that the character Dorien was referring to in the television comedy programme *Birds of a Feather* when she said about suburban women that they have all that they want but nothing that they need.

Perhaps today you are searching for a life worth living. It may be out of a sense of dissatisfaction: a dissatisfaction that was born out of tragedy, out of having it all but still wanting something. What we need to be aware of, according to Solomon, is that in regard to this world, what it has to offer will never give us what we are searching for.

Why? Why is it so? That question Solomon unfortunately does not answer. Not here, anyway. Perhaps the answer is found in the description that the philosopher Plato gives to humankind:

We are but leaky jars.

We need not so much to have something poured into us as to be fixed.

The benefits of his discovery

Those of you who have seen the film *The Truman Show* will know that Truman began to realise that what was around him was not as real as he thought. Rather than living in a lovely seaside town, he was in fact living on a giant television set. Those around him were nothing more than actors who were there to help him live out his life before a global television audience. Unfortunately, he was the only one who did not know that.

As he began to understand that things were not as they seemed, Truman decided to journey to that which was outside his immediate life setting. A difficult journey? Yes. But a necessary one.

Did he discover what he was looking for? Yes. Although the director only takes us as far as Truman arriving at the edge of the giant stage, the suggestion is that it was there that he found what he was looking for.

When Solomon came to the end of his journey it was with the same sort of hopes as Truman – that the discoveries he had made would lead to his release. All through his search Solomon has adventured as a man who is thirsty for life worth living. All through his quest he has viewed life as if he were a man imprisoned. As he comes to the close, he comes perhaps with a hope of final release.

Unfortunately, what he discovers is that all the wisdom he has gained does not affect his imprisonment – in the short term, anyway. Whereas Truman's journey led him to a stage door that would lead him out into the real world, for Solomon there was no door.

The fact that life was not worth living under the sun was for Solomon thoroughly depressing. In fact, says Solomon, all it did was give him further sorrow and grief:

> For with much wisdom comes much sorrow;
> the more knowledge, the more grief.

The realisation, the twinkling, that promised so much actually added to his chains in that it declared to him that there was no way out.

Is it any wonder that the philosopher commits suicide? Is there anything so pitiful as a person who knows that life is meaningless, and can do nothing about it? It's like being a child in an enormous shopping mall, lost and aware of the fact.

What is particularly important to note here is that knowledge, the currency of the nineties and the heir to

God's throne in the twenty-first century, is not able to deliver us from our sense of being lost in the universe. Alvin Toffler in his book *Powershift*,[1] the third in his trilogy of books on the future, talks about how knowledge will be the commodity of this century. It will be what you know, or what information you can get your hands on, which will be more important than who you know or how much money you have. What Solomon tells us is that in regard to the quest for life worth living even knowledge is futile:

> *Then I applied myself to the understanding of wisdom, and also of madness and folly, but I learned that this, too, is a chasing after the wind.*

Educationalists might tell us that we need the three R's – reading, writing and arithmetic. Others would say that we really need four R's – reading, writing, arithmetic and respect. What Solomon tells us is that when you add them all together they actually equal another R. Redundant. At the end of the day, says Solomon, it is all meaningless. Meaningless.

Conclusion

Within this chapter we have been looking at a man on a quest, a quest to answer one of life's fundamental questions. Is life worth living? As we have studied this man we have seen that he is more than qualified to take us on our adventure. He is a man of wisdom, study and experience. With regard to finding buried treasure, we

---

[1] Alvin Toffler, *Powershift: Knowledge, Wealth, and Violence at the Edge of the 21st Century* (Bantam, 1990).

have been greatly disappointed, as through our quest we have discovered that life is not worth living. Under the sun, anyway. What is more, Solomon has informed us that because of this finding even the information that we have gained will, in fact, be of no positive use to us.

To finish this chapter, I would like to put forward a few more questions. Is that it, then? Is that all there is to say about life worth living? Or is there something else to be said?

My opinion and the teachings of the Bible are that there is more to be said. If one reads between the lines, one can see that Solomon actually says as much in this chapter. If there is nothing, nothing under the sun, that can give meaning to life, then perhaps our only hope is above it?

If a person had all that was visible, but was still empty, perhaps that which would fill that person is invisible.

Why oh why do we have this yearning to find meaning if there is none to be found? Where did it come from? Why is it within? Why will it not go away? Why have we not evolved on from it?

If what Solomon says about life under the sun is true, then why did he go to all this effort and thought to record for us its emptiness? Because he wanted to tell us the truth about life in a way that would lead to life.

There exists within our world a false hope. Sartre says it is something that we will not let go of. It's a hope that expresses itself in such phrases as 'There's light at the end of the tunnel' – Solomon wants us to know that there is not. If there is, it is only the headlights of an oncoming train. 'Our boat will come in' – we need to realise that it sank a long time ago. 'Things are not as bad as they seem' – they are worse. 'Every cloud has a silver lining' – the silk lining of a coffin's padding.

In answer to my friend's question, I say, 'Yes, life is worth living.' But we must stop looking for its true meaning under the sun and start looking for it under heaven.

Chapter 2

God on ... twenty-first-century life

I want to introduce you to an old friend of mine named Ronald. Ronald is thirty-eight years of age. He's about to become the new managing director of a large financial institution. For fun he drives a Volkswagen GTi and has recently bought a four-bedroom house in a much-sought-after area of London. He is single and at this time has no steady girlfriend. He regards himself, still, as an eighties yuppie.

His interests? Money, his career, sex and pleasure. Fun and leisure play a big part in his life. He likes music, parties, sports, entertainment, holidays, drinking and romances. He dreams of making love to Lara Croft – hopefully on his next holiday to the Caribbean. And, because he is a child of his age, the microwave age, he expects such things immediately. In the words of the late Freddie Mercury, he wants it all and he wants it now.

What does he value? Materialism for him is the sign of success. That is why he has such an urge to make more and more money. He can remember having to tighten up a bit in the recession, but that was some time ago. Now it's back to having a blast while you last. He also believes in the importance of the individual, particularly the right to personal freedom. Anything should be allowed to go. If it feels good then he should be able to do it. He also believes that he has a right to believe whatever he likes. So does everyone else; that is, as long as their views don't infringe on him. He also believes in personal survival. Therefore he thinks that the Government should get on with the job of saving the planet. His purpose in life, his mission statement, is to reach the top and consume the most and die with the most toys.

As far as his hopes are concerned, he hopes for a quality life, which he understands as consisting of happiness, fun, acceptance, stability and security. He sees these being fulfilled through money, success, health, career and possessions. He believes that contentment is but a credit card away – American Express, of course – and that quality of life is dependent upon what you have in your piggy bank.

What about his fears? He fears emptiness, failure, rejection, loneliness, illness and unemployment. His two great nightmares are that when he is old no one is going to want to listen to him and that one day he is going to die. He very rarely talks about either of these concerns.

What about his attitude to the church? He rejects and ignores it, as do so many of his contemporaries. Some might go so far as to say that he doesn't even know that it exists, let alone what for. However, in saying that, we should not then conclude that he is not interested in spiritual things. Ronald is someone who has a deep interest in several spiritual themes.

To society, Ronald is a normal, successful, going-places acquaintance of (in Britain) New Labour. He is someone whose life is definitely together. He is someone who believes in the inevitability of progress, yet who enjoys antiques, who is searching for the hero inside himself, which he is not sure he will find.

What I want to do in this chapter is look to see what Solomon has to say to Ronald regarding life, to find out what this famous king has to say to someone living in the fast lane of the twenty-first century.

Solomon has three things to say to Ronald from his journal.

Solomon's testimony on what society says makes for life

By the word testimony, we mean Solomon's eyewitness account, his experience of life, his story. Now, as he tells his story he wants us, his readers, to know that this testimony is not that of some non-participatory observer, armchair critic or potential *Telly Addicts* contestant. What he is about to say comes from his own personal experiences; not the experiences of others, observed and then commented on. They are his experiences. This is like Jeremy Guscott, a rugby player, reporting live from Landsdown Road. It is not Des Lynham, a television commentator, talking from the studio.

What is more, from what we read, these are not the comments of one who is down on his luck, or, as some of my friends would say, a 'Norm'. 'Norm' is short for Norman, and means one of life's no-hopers. This is someone who has gone and got a life.

Within his testimony Solomon tells us about two things: everything that he has tried in his pursuit of life and the results of his activities.

What did he try?
What did he try? Firstly, he tells us that he tried enjoyment. Solomon lived in an age where people believed 'If it feels good, I should do it.' Sensation seeking was the way of

the day. Eros or sensual pleasure was the deity that people worshipped.

> *Come now, I will test you with pleasure to find out*
> *what is good.*

He tried laughter, joking with the lads, watching the best sitcoms, hearing the best stand-up comedians. He took his family to EuroDisney every day.

He tried old-fashioned community togetherness. He threw parties for 10,000–20,000 people daily. We lived in Scotland at a time when big commemorations of the 200-year anniversary of Robert Burns' death were being planned and rumour had it that Pavarotti would sing in the park. Solomon says he did such things every day.

He became a connoisseur of fine wines:

> *I tried cheering myself with wine …*

Solomon was no lager lout. 'Not me,' he says. 'I went for the quality stuff.'

He had a harem all for himself. He was the original Hugh Hefner. He denied himself nothing his eyes desired. Furthermore, he got involved in great architectural, horticultural and agricultural projects:

> *I undertook great projects: I built houses for myself and*
> *planted vineyards. I made gardens and parks and planted all*
> *kinds of fruit trees in them. I made reservoirs to water groves*
> *of flourishing trees.*

He even tried materialism:

> *I amassed silver and gold for myself, and the treasure of kings*
> *and provinces.*

He became greater than any man who has ever lived.

He even tried the entertainment business. One of my friends is working hard with his band to break into the music scene on a national level. Solomon says, 'I went that way. I employed singers to perform.' Elsewhere we read how he got involved in song writing, perhaps writing the songs that these singers would sing. He wrote over a thousand songs. Who knows, some of them might have gone to number one. 'You name it,' says Solomon. 'I did it. There was nothing I did not do.'

> *I refused my heart no pleasure.*

He might even have applied for the post of spiritual adviser to a former manager of the England football team

What did he find?

And what did he find? The same conclusion as he presents in the previous chapter:

> *everything was meaningless, a chasing after the wind ...*

Oh, there was a delight in trying to attain the things that he attained, but in the cold light of day that which he had was empty.

> *My heart took delight in all my work,*
> *and this was the reward for all my labour.*
> *Yet when I surveyed all that my hands had done*
> *and what I had toiled to achieve,*
> *everything was meaningless, a chasing after the wind;*
> *nothing was gained under the sun.*

Several years ago my wife Sarah and I had to change our car. Since we were short on cash, we were really restricted in the type of car that we could have. We worked out how much we could afford and then looked around. Unfortunately, we had no luck. Sarah's dad, being the kind of man he was, also looked for us. He found a car down where he lived, which he thought would be OK. He got it for us and then said that he would drive it to us.

I know absolutely nothing about cars, so although he told us what it was it meant nothing to us. Well, on the day that he was travelling up, we were filled with excitement. For the limited amount of money we had, he had managed to get an E-reg car, just two years old. The fact that it was so new and cost so little money should have set the alarm bells ringing, but it didn't. We were going to have an E-reg car. Incredible.

We were, to say the least, disappointed when we saw it. For we had, in fact, become owners of a Yugo! Now, I don't know if that smacks of bad luck where you live, but it did for me. You know, I got so much cheek at one point that I could only drive it at night. These were some of the comments I got about my car. 'What do you call a Yugo with no roof?' 'A skip.' 'What do you call a Yugo doing fifty on the motorway?' 'A miracle.' It promised so much yet delivered so little.

'That', says Solomon, 'is my conclusion on life.'

The supporters of West Ham United Football Club chant that they are forever blowing bubbles. Life, says Solomon, is a continual striving after those bubbles and the discovery upon catching one of them that they are empty, meaningless. It's like being a joy rider for whom everything goes wrong. One minute you think everything is going well, this is living, but then you lose control, getting yourself, and usually someone else, hurt. It's like living life the morning after the party. Getting ready for the party was exciting and being at the party was great, but next morning it was coffee and aspirin.

There was an article in a British newspaper some time ago entitled 'Trading Places'. The write-up was all about the exploits of a couple of people who had changed jobs with either their friends or kin for a day and then commented on what it was like. Solomon tells us in his autobiography that he traded places with everyone one would like to trade places with. His conclusion is that one shouldn't bother.

The first thing, then, that Solomon does is to give Ronald exclusive rights to his story on what the world says makes for life. His conclusion? It is meaningless, a chasing after the wind.

Solomon's test for life

A couple of years ago Bob Paisley died. Bob Paisley, as the news reports told us, was one of Britain's greatest football managers. Evidence of his greatness was to be seen in the number of trophies that Liverpool won under his leadership, either in Europe or at home, in the league or cup competitions. What was particularly noteworthy about his funeral was that as well as acknowledging the man's achievements, many were very generous in their commending of the man's character.

As we all know, the fate of Bob Paisley is the fate that is common to humankind. What Solomon goes on to tell us is that the fate of Bob Paisley is not only the fate of us all but more importantly it is the test that all of us must sit. It is, according to Solomon, the test of life that ultimately determines whether one's life has been worth living or not.

This test of life – death – is an often-paddled stream in Solomon's autobiography. If you read the book you will find that he returns to it again and again. But then that's not surprising, is it. If one is looking at life under the sun, between the two extremes of birth and death, you have to look at death quite a lot.

Perhaps one of the reasons that people today have problems with life is that we have tried to remove the reality of death from the public view, which is really silly when you think about it. As Euripides the poet said:

> *it is the debt that we must all pay.*

And as George Bernard Shaw said:

> *The statistic that we can all be sure of is that one*
> *out of one die.*

As the Bible says:

> *it is appointed for men to die once ...* (NKJV)

The French essayist Montaigne has an interesting perspective on philosophy and death. He says that 'philosophy is nothing more than helping a man to prepare himself for death'.

Tests

As well as telling us that death is the test of life, what Solomon also does for us is to conduct some experiments against this test on our behalf. What he does is look at how wisdom, wealth and fame fare in the light of the graveside.

As far as wisdom is concerned, we are told that 'it is far better to be wise than foolish', but at the end of the day does it really matter, for the same fate awaits both?

> *Then I thought in my heart,*
> *'The fate of the fool will overtake me also.*
> *What then do I gain by being wise?'*
> *I said in my heart, 'This too is meaningless.'*

> *For the wise man, like the fool,*
> *will not be long remembered;*
> *in days to come both will be forgotten.*
> *Like the fool, the wise man too must die!*

So then, what about my friends' concern to ensure that their child goes to the best schools, even if that means moving home? At the end of the day, says Solomon, does it really matter?

We must also look at wealth and how that compares against the test of life, death. At the end of the day this too, says Solomon, 'is meaningless', for three reasons:
Firstly, I cannot keep what I have obtained:

> *I hated all things I had toiled for under the sun, because I*
> *must leave them ...*

A writer in the *Wall Street Journal* referred to money as:

> *an article which may be used as a universal passport to*
> *everywhere except heaven, and as a universal provider of*
> *everything except happiness.*

The problem is, as one Jewish proverb says, 'There are no pockets in shrouds.' It's useless – I can't take it to heaven.
Secondly, what is worse, I cannot determine how my money will be spent when I am gone:

> *And who knows whether he will be a wise man or a fool? Yet*
> *he will have control over all the work into which I have poured*
> *my effort and skill under the sun.*

It could so easily be wasted. Solomon's son realised his father's fears by squandering the old man's money.

Thirdly, because I cannot take my money to the grave with me or determine how it is spent when I am gone, I cannot enjoy it now:

So my heart began to despair over all my toilsome labour
under the sun.

I am brought to despair because of the fact that I cannot take it with me and because I don't know how it will be spent when I am gone.

Later on in his autobiography Solomon is going to concentrate on the subject of money. Some people believe that money brings satisfaction, money solves all your problems, money can give you peace of mind, money provides security. What Solomon shows us here is that such beliefs are heresy, it's all a myth. Contrary to some people's views, money is not a god.

How should we regard fame? This question is perhaps particularly pertinent in the light of the great admiration given to Bob Paisley. At the end of the day it too is meaningless:

For the wise man, like the fool, will not be long remembered;
in days to come both will be forgotten.

Solomon records for us his feelings after obtaining such findings:

I hated life …

The problem was, as the French humanist Voltaire says:

I hate life and yet I am afraid to die.

The story is told of a businessman who was offered a great amount of money for his company. It was such a good deal that he just had to take it. Now, rather than start another business or look for another job, this man decided finally to take that retirement that he had been talking about. For all of this man's working life he had acted wisely and sensibly. He had invested well, he had developed his business slowly and surely, he had been a textbook example of how to grow your own little empire and gold mine. After all these years, now was the time to settle back and live in the good of it.

Unfortunately, so the story goes, all did not turn out well for this fellow. Tragically, on the night of his big retirement do, he had a heart attack and died.

What I find interesting about this story, and the reason I mention it, is the critique of the storyteller on this man's life. Jesus, the man who told the story, said that this man had in fact died not a rich man but rather a fool.

The reason for his judgement? Despite the fact that the man had lots of wealth this side of eternity, he had none for the other side. In living for himself, in seeing his god as possessions, in denying the reality of the life to come, he had never invested in the bank that determines how we shall live in the life to come after death – in eternity. He had failed the test of life, something Solomon says will happen to Ronald, perhaps to all of us, if we do not bank with the right establishment.

Solomon tells the truth about life

Before moving to where we now live, I went to work as the leader of a church. One of the first things that I did was to have the church secretary come round and tell me about how the church operated. What went on? Who did what? As you can imagine, the meeting was a long one.

At the end of our meeting – we were in my study at the time – the secretary and I bowed our heads and prayed together. I prayed first and then the secretary. When he prayed I noticed a slight hesitation at one point in his prayer but thought nothing of it. A couple of weeks later I found out why the secretary had hesitated.

After he had started to pray he felt something on his knee. Obviously not knowing me that well, he initially thought that I was just identifying with him. But then he felt it again, higher up his leg. It was at this point that he had hesitated. What he had thought at that point he was unwilling to say! What he discovered on opening his eyes was that my cat had jumped on to his knee and was settling down.

The third thing that Solomon says to Ronald is what he saw when he has opened his eyes. Not what he felt moving up his leg, but what he saw in regard to enjoying life.

It is important to note that it is at this juncture that Solomon changes the venue for his deliberations. Whereas under the sun has been his world-view for the first two points that he has made to Ronald, under heaven is the framework within which he makes his final point – it is a view of life that includes God.

What is the truth about life?

Firstly, there is nothing inherent in a person that makes it possible for him or her to extract enjoyment and purpose from the things he or she does:

> *A man can do nothing to eat and drink and find*
> *satisfaction in his work.*

We are, says Solomon, in the same state as John D. Rockefeller was at the end of his life. Despite the fact that he had millions of dollars, due to his physical condition he could eat but a pauper's amount of food.

Secondly, what is the truth about life? It is that enjoyment is God's gift:

> *for without him, who can eat and find enjoyment?*

You can have it all, yet without God you have nothing. You can have nothing, and yet with God have it all. Possessing the ability to enjoy is more important that possessing possessions to enjoy. And that ability comes from God.

How does God give us the ability to enjoy life? He spikes our lives. Have you ever been to a party where someone's drinks have been spiked, when some other substance has been added, usually without that person knowing? The difference it makes to the person who is drinking it is quite considerable.

Many years ago there was a particular group of lads who always went out together whenever there was something to celebrate. They were a rather traditional bunch and so they always went to the same place. It was there that they saw first-hand the difference that spiking drinks could have on a person.

Through the course of an evening they saw a quiet, dour type of person become the life and soul of the party. From being one who sat in the corner in a permanent sulk, he became someone who decided that he would take on the role of 'The Leader of the Pack' in Gary Glitter's song. It's quite a sight seeing one of your more conservative friends standing on a chair miming to a song, let alone climbing on to a table and walking along it seeing if he could dodge all the food. He went wild. All because someone had foolishly added something to his drink.

In the same way that someone spiked his drink, so giving him the time of his life, so God, says the Bible, wants to spike our lives so that we might have the ability to enjoy life. Alcohol has nothing to do with it.

What's the truth about life, asks Solomon? It is that joy is a gift of God.

Conclusion

Let's bring this all together and draw some conclusions. One day when Christianity's founder, Jesus, was heading off to a meeting in Jerusalem, he was approached by a man the Bible calls the Rich Young Ruler. The reason for the young man's approach was that he had a question that he wanted Jesus to answer. His question was, 'What must I do to inherit eternal life?' – or, in this context, 'What must I do to have a life worth living?'

What is interesting about this man is that he comes to Jesus as one who has everything. He is young, he is rich, he is powerful! Everything that you and I dream of having, everything that you and I work to get, everything that our contemporaries play the lottery for, he has, and yet he comes to Jesus. Interestingly, the young man even displays a hint of moral and religious character.

And what is Jesus' answer? What must you do to have a life worth living? 'You must go sell everything you have and then give it to the poor and then come follow me.'

What we are talking about here is giving up everything to Jesus' control; getting rid of that which is an alternative idol. This answer of Jesus is the answer that the Bible gives to all of us today who might be asking the question 'What must I do to have a life worth living?'

At first glance one might describe such an answer as a bit harsh and thoughtless. However, as we have seen, this

would be far from the truth. You see, Jesus' perspective on
life would have been the same as Solomon's. That which
the rich young ruler had was meaningless. He already
knew that; that's why he came to Jesus. In the light of
death he was failing. It is only with God that he could
have a life worth living. Therefore he must follow Jesus.
Jesus' statement that he is the way to God was actually a
very attractive offer.

Solomon, although not identifying Christ as 'the way',
comes to the same conclusion:

> *To the man who pleases him, God gives wisdom,*
> *knowledge and happiness ...*

You might feel that your life is like one of those 3D pictures
– you just can't get the picture together. Solomon has put
the pieces together for us. We need God in our lives.

In the next chapter of his diary Solomon identifies for us
how we are all searching for something. Unfortunately,
many of us are unable to identify what it is, or how to
obtain it. What we have seen here is how Solomon says
we can be satisfied.

Chapter 3

God on ... time, eternity, injustice and death

In the last chapter I introduced you to a friend of mine called Ronald. I want to begin this chapter by telling you a little about his brother, Paul.

In some ways Ronald and Paul are very similar: they both wish they had more free time; they are both working hard at developing their careers; they share similar hopes and fears. What marks them apart is their attitude to God. Both of them are aware of God, Ronald in the sense that there might be a God – though this belief is theoretical and not experiential (he lives as though there were no God). Paul, on the other hand, not only intellectually believes in God, he is also trying experientially to work out his belief in his daily life.

Now, what I want to do in this chapter is look at what Solomon has to say to us about the lives of Ronald and Paul. As we do that, I want to ask the question, 'Are you a Ronald or a Paul?'

Are you doing time or having the time of your life?

Several years ago the scientist Stephen Hawking published a book entitled *A Brief History of Time*,[2] in which he talks

---

2 Stephen W. Hawking, *A Brief History of Time: From the Big Bang to Black Holes* (Bantam, 1988).

about various categories of time. For those of you who haven't read the book, he talks about cosmological time, thermodynamic time and other such difficult concepts.

Solomon, in Ecclesiastes 3, wanting to make his thoughts available to all, gives us a layperson's guide to a lifetime, what you and I would expect to find in the simplest of daily newspapers.

What he says is that life is made up of seasons. These seasons are ingredients in the life cycle of a man or woman. Biologists tell us that there are seven ages of man; Solomon says that there are twenty-eight possible seasons to pass through, seasons that rhythmically ebb and flow in and out of our lives.

We are also told that as these seasons ebb and flow we will find that they have the potential to complement and oppose each other. Hence it is possible to go through several positive and complementary seasons, such as planting, scattering stones and embracing. It is also possible to go through several negative seasons, such as uprooting, tearing down and throwing away.

In addition, it is also possible to go through seasons that contradict one another. For instance, a positive season that is marked by laughter can be followed by a negative season that is marked by weeping.

The significant point that Solomon is making in these fourteen pairs of contrasts, which is the emphasis of this section, is that such seasons are outside our control. They are pre-determined times. We get that from the meaning of the Hebrew word for 'time'. It infers a set, diaried date. We didn't choose the time to be born and we don't in most cases choose the time to die.

Now, what Solomon asks in this best-known part of Ecclesiastes is does such knowledge of our pre-determined seasons make you feel as if you're doing time in jail or enjoying time at the fairground? Is your cry that of Mick Jagger – 'I can't get no satisfaction' – or that of Patrick Swayze in the film *Dirty Dancing* – 'I'm having the time of my life?' It's an important question. For Ronald, what we are told is that such pre-set seasons prove to make time a tyrant. Why? There is for Ronald no control over his life. He is at best a slave to fate. It is a wasted effort for him to try and improve his lot as he is forced to dance to a tune not of his own choosing. There is to this rhythmic poem a repressive, oppressive beat for Ronald. He is not the master of his own destiny, but rather finds himself in a changing world in which he does not determine the changes. In many senses life becomes a bloody and difficult time.

If you ever saw the film *Clockwise* with John Cleese you will remember that in it he played a headmaster who did everything not only by the book but also by the clock. However, one day, a very important day in his life, our headmaster found that nothing was going by the clock. Try as he might to set an agenda, try as he might to plan things out, try as he might to devise a strategy or programme to sort things out, he could not control the order of events that he went through. Such, says Solomon, is how Ronald feels about his life. Such knowledge caused singer Jon Bon Jovi to say of life:

> Let's face it, this is an ugly world, a filthy place to be.
> It's a bunch of whores.[3]

For many people, life is like being in the same capsized boat as the yachtsmen Tony Bullimore, being blown here and there by winds that one has no control over, with the

---

[3] Martin Wroe (ed.), *God: What the Critics Say* (Spire, 1992).

knowledge that in your predicament there is no Australian navy to rescue you.

Such knowledge of one's fated life provokes Ronald to ask the question 'What, then, do I gain from my labour?' If the course of one's life is determined by chance, what's the point?

As for Paul, what does such an awareness of the seasons of life do for him? It causes him to make one of the most optimistic yet truthful statements in the book of Ecclesiastes – that in time all things will be made beautiful. That in the right time, all things will become good. This belief is what provoked the friends of Brian in *Monty Python's Life of Brian* to sing 'Always look on the bright side of life' at the cross.

Do notice those words 'all things'. Paul believes that in time everything that we go through – and let's be honest, he knows that we go through some really poohy things in our lives – will become good. Paul says that such knowledge causes him to believe that one day there will be a rightness to everything. To illnesses endured – yes. To unemployment – yes. To seemingly undeserved tragedy – yes. To the loss of a loved one – yes. Paul tells us that he has such confidence because he knows that we live to a pre-determined plan.

For those of you who are familiar with the Bible, you will note the seeds here for the comments of the Apostle Paul that all things work together for good. Where does such confidence come from? Well, Solomon tells us in his words that God will make all things beautiful in their time.

You see, whereas Ronald saw fate as the determiner of the seasons of life, Paul sees the hands of God as the determiner. What he experiences are not the ad hoc,

un-agended, by-chance seasons of life. They are the pre-
determined, God-planned occasions in his life, which God
has chosen specifically for him. Paul is expressing faith here
in the first-ever Dr Who, the original Time Lord, the God
of heaven and earth. Michael Ball sang that 'love changes
everything'. That is Paul's conclusion. The fact that God
loves him gives a meaning and context to all that he goes
through.

Does it solve for him the riddle of life? No. There will
be times when he will not understand why he is going
through what he is going through. It will still hurt, but he
knows that one day, whether on this side or the other, all
will be beautiful.

Several months ago in an episode of the British television
series *Ballykissangel* we were given an example of one of
the tragic paradoxes of life. Niamh, who had so happily
become pregnant, miscarried, and a girl who had given
birth but who didn't want the child dumped her baby on
the priest's doorstep.

You know, we have friends who are desperate for children, but who can't get pregnant. Try as they might, be
they potentially the best parents ever, they cannot conceive.
We know of other people who are without doubt the worst
possible parents who can't stop conceiving. It's so unfair,
isn't it? And then there are those who lose their child,
whether early in pregnancy or in infancy. Solomon tells
us that the knowledge that God makes all things beautiful
in their time might not take the pain away, but it will give
us hope for tomorrow. In regard to your lifetime, asks
Solomon, how do you see it?

The last words of Spock to Jim in one of the Star Trek
films were 'Jim, enjoy the journey.' The question Solomon
asks us is, are we enjoying ours? The question is answered

by being a Paul instead of a Ronald; being one who incorporates God into life as opposed to one who doesn't.

Tell me, says Solomon, what's your story? Are you doing time in prison or having the time of your life at the fairground?

Eternity – is it unfathomable or inspirational?

For those of you who are fans of the film hero Indiana Jones, you will know that the last movie that Harrison Ford made was all about Indie's attempt to find the Holy Grail, this being the cup that Jesus supposedly drank out of at the Last Supper. What added impetus to the search was the belief that whoever drank from the cup would inherit immortality. It was one heck of an adventure getting there.

One of the reasons why I like this film, *Indiana Jones and the Last Crusade*, is that it reflects and expresses an appetite that is within me, and which I believe is in everyone – the appetite to touch the eternal, that which is immortal, to join oneself with the future. That's why I like the Star Wars films as well. There is a desire to be joined with the eternal force, to be the next Luke Skywalker, to fulfil my destiny.

I suppose that's why many people are into the television sci-fi series *The X Files* – because it offers a possibility of understanding the unknown, that which is out there.

This desire to understand what is ahead of us and to be joined with it has been around since time immemorial. Today, horoscopes are sold on the basis of it.

What you might not know is that the reason for this appetite is that there is within each one of us a sense of eternity. Of all the animals, it is only humankind that is curious about the future. We have within us an eternal itch to know about tomorrow. To quote the captain of the *Starship Enterprise*, we want 'to boldly go where no man has gone before'. It makes us feel as if we have all the time in the world. It prevents us from feeling as if we are completely at home here on the earth. It is what drives us to the stars and to see every movie about aliens. Sure, at times this quest shouts louder than at other times, but if we think back over our lives what we will be aware of is that it has always been calling us on. Or is it perhaps calling us home?

When it comes to eternity, are you a Star Wars Wookie: one who finds eternity unfathomable, an unquenchable thirst? Or an Obi-Wan Kenobi: one who not only understands the force, but who is utilising it? Are you a Ronald or a Paul?

Are you a Ronald? For Ronald, eternity is unfathomable, unquenchable. Bruce Springsteen sang about everybody having a hungry heart, and that is Ronald's conclusion. He just can't satisfy this eternal appetite within him. He feels that eternity is like a tin of sardines, in that we are all looking for the key.

Ronald has done much to quench this thirst. Thinking initially that it was a human hunger, he sought to live the men-behaving-badly life – drinks with the lads; party time all the time. Then he tried the image of the American sitcom *Friends* – clean cut, good job, nice girlfriend, nice life. When he realised that that didn't do it, he tried Shirley MacClain's approach of trying to find the god within you. Then it was yoga down at the local leisure centre. He got into green issues and saving the planet, looking for contentment in becoming one with Mother Earth. Solomon tells us that Ronald, still unable to find what he needs, has decided to try and get the best out of every day as long as his life lasts, since when it is over, that's the end.

For Ronald, eternity is an unsolvable puzzle.

For Paul, with his belief in God, eternity is neither unfathomable nor unquenchable; rather it is inspirational. Why? Well, very simply, because Paul sees God in it. He is in history. It is His-story:

> *Whatever is has already been, and what will be*
> *has been before;*
> *and God will call the past to account.*

He is at work in the world today:

> *I know that everything God does will endure for ever; nothing*
> *can be added to it and nothing taken from it. God does it so*
> *that men will revere him.*

He is in Paul's life:

> *That everyone may eat and drink, and find satisfaction in all*
> *his toil – this is the gift of God.*

He is in Paul's tomorrows: he will make all things beautiful in his time.

The way that eternity proves to be inspirational for Paul can be seen in the following three ways.

Firstly, the way it gives him a right relationship with God. Paul tells us that he fears God. To fear God does not mean to be afraid of him in a debilitating way. Rather, it means to have such an appreciation of him that one gives him the proper respect and response. It is the recipe for having the best and most rewarding relationship with him. Paul claims to have that type of relationship, the potential of it, anyway.

Secondly, eternity is inspirational for Paul in that it causes him to live life well. Paul sees that because life is more than that which we have this side, the best way to live life is to invest in his eternal tomorrow by doing good to others. Furthermore, because he knows that his eternity is secure, he can enjoy his lot now. He says:

I know that there is nothing better for men than to be happy and to do good while they live.

What perhaps best illustrates the way in which eternity is an inspiration for Paul can be seen in the way that he will die.

Several years ago I got talking to a friend of mine called Joan about her job. Joan has a very interesting job: she is a nurse at a hospital that cares for those who are terminally ill. Joan works on the ward where people go when they are about to die. In talking to Joan about her job and what she had seen, she made a very interesting comparison between those who die with faith and those who don't. The difference, she said, was not in that one group experienced pain and the other didn't – sometimes there was severe pain. The difference was that when a Christian died he or she normally died peacefully, but when someone who wasn't a Christian died there wasn't that element of peace, either in the patient or his or her family. Solomon's explanation for this is that for some eternity is unfathomable, whilst for others it is inspirational. Paul sees it as inspirational. What Solomon asks us is, is that how we see it?

The injustices of life – are you resigned or awaiting God's justice?

In the newspaper recently there was the story of a lawyer who had decided to withdraw from the legal profession.

The reason that the lawyer gave for his decision was that he felt that he could no longer stomach what he saw going on. In his mind it was no longer a matter of whether you had a good case or not, but rather how many financial strings a client was able to pull for the best lawyer to be present. What he also struggled with was the lack of justice that he found: sentences often did not equate with the wickedness of the crime; the scandalous shift in values meant that now you could get longer for theft than murder.

In Solomon's day it was no different. As he looked around his world he saw wickedness and injustice abounding. He saw traders who sold T-shirts at ridiculous prices whilst only paying their employees a pittance. He saw a Government that wanted to fund a new boat for the Nile that would cost millions, which could go to housing for the poor. He saw a wicked man's family plan to make another killing, though this time financial, on the life story of their dad, while his victim's families got only suffering.

What Solomon is asking us is, in seeing such things, how do you feel? What is your response to it all?

Solomon tells us that, for Ronald, the feelings were of anger and resignation. He saw the injustices of life, the unfairness of life, but what could he do? Whether because he feared risking his own life or whether because he felt he could not make a difference, Solomon records for us how Ronald simply notes that such inequalities exist. Tragically, in the end Ronald became a victim of bitterness.

And Paul, what was his response? Interestingly, his was one of anger and patience. He too saw the injustices of life and was appalled. But what he also saw was a time when God would bring about judgement on such wickedness.

When that time was, he did not know, but he knew that it would come.

Let me say that those who have grasped God's timing have been some of the greatest reformers the world has ever known.

When it comes to injustice and wickedness, says Solomon, how do you view it? How do you feel?

The grave – is it a dead end or the end of the beginning?

One day, almost everyone reading this is going to have a Christian minister say the words about 'ashes to ashes, dust to dust' over them at their funeral. It might be at a crematorium, it might be at a graveside, our coffin might be surrounded with loved ones or there might be very few who have come to say farewell. On that day, what I want to ask is, is this act of committal going to mark a dead end for you or only the end of the beginning?

Death is an often-paddled stream in Ecclesiastes. The reason for this is that Solomon saw it as a door that will open for all of us and a door through which all of us will walk.

In Chapter 2 I commented on how death is the one non-negotiable of life. It is the horrific test of life. It is capable of making the most famous, the richest and the wisest person also the most miserable this side of death.

When it comes to death you might have the same attitude to it as Woody Allen. He once said, 'I don't mind dying, I just don't want to be there when it happens.' Or perhaps your view is the same as that of Groucho Marx! He was asked once what it felt like to be ninety years old, with all the things that go with old age: memory loss, lack of strength, loss of hair. His answer: 'It's better than the alternative.' Whatever your view, the reality of it is that all of us will one day die.

What Solomon asks in this final section of Ecclesiastes 3 is, when you contemplate your death, how do you see it?

In Solomon's mind, when it comes to death there seem to be two possible perspectives to take. You can see it as the end of the line or a platform to another destination. Which view do you hold?

What Solomon goes on to tell us is that the characteristics of both perspectives are quite incredible.

Solomon is looking at our perspectives on death because, just like any good life assurance salesperson, he wants to ensure not only that we are aware of the stark facts about after we have gone but also that we take out the necessary cover.

As in all the other contradictory perspectives that Solomon has been looking at, the perspective is determined by whether you incorporate God into your world-view or not.

As I have already identified, Ronald is our intellectual agnostic with the lifestyle of an atheist. What Solomon tells us is that, for Ronald, the thought of his death gives rise to mourning.

The reasons for this are twofold. Firstly, because it shows him that he is no different from the animals, therefore robbing him of all dignity:

> *Man's fate is like that of the animals; the same fate awaits them both: As one dies, so dies the other. All have the same breadth; man has no advantage over the animal.*

For Ronald, the thought of the grave also gives rise to mourning because it causes all people to be equal. Within its grasp no one is nobler than any other. With the same end as the snail or the snake, our purpose becomes as meaningless as the animals'. Yes, there is a purpose, but so little a purpose.

What makes matters worse for Ronald is that death is not only the great apartheid destroyer; it is also for him a great time of uncertainty. He has absolutely no assurance of what lies beyond death or of where he is going. It is marked by hopelessness and despair.

Who knows if the spirit of man rises upward and if the spirit of the animal goes down into the earth?

One of the British national daily papers ran a series of articles recently on what is beyond death. Incorporating the after-death experiences of several people who were then medically brought back to life, they speculated as to what existed beyond the big bright light.

At the end of the day their opinions can be at best as good as Ronald's. They do not know. They do not know if there is anything, and if there is anything what that anything is.

Recently the funeral of a very prominent man was held in a town in South Wales. During his lifetime this man had built up a thriving business with offices in several other towns. He was known as a good man who worked hard. You could be sure to find him in his office before 7 a.m. He was a man who loved his wife and who cared deeply for her, a man who did all that he could to ease her in her own illnesses. Even in the last week of life he arranged to have their house decorated so that there was one less thing for her to worry about.

This man arranged to have his funeral at the local town hall. With no belief in God, for him death was the end. What a tragic, despairing scene – a funeral service that was held with no hope. There was no hope of resurrection, of meeting with his family again. It was the end and there was no more.

This is Ronald's perspective, the reality that he flirts and fights with. What Solomon asks is, is this yours?

Again, Paul is someone who is not only open to the concept of God but is daily seeking to filter him into his life. For him, therefore, death is not a dead end but rather it carries with it a time of great expectancy.

The reason for this is that Paul understands what death is. It is not a dead end but rather only the end of the beginning:

> I also thought, 'As for men, God tests them so that they may see that they are like the animals.'

Death is nothing more than a test. From what we read of death elsewhere in the Bible, it is an entry exam to that which is far better and which lies ahead. In the more recent part of the Bible, the New Testament, the author of 1 Corinthians notes how, in regard to every one of us, death is but a doorway to the eternity that is beyond.

Now, in regard to this eternity, what we are also told is that there are two destinations. Our standing at death determines which of these destinations will be allocated to us. What the New Testament goes on to intimate, quite surprisingly, is that our standing at death is not determined by our good works, a religious upbringing, a moral life, or anything else which one might be able to boast of as a human achievement. Rather, our standing or rating is determined by what we have done with regard to God's son Jesus Christ. Our acceptance of him and commitment to following him through the course of our life gives us automatic acceptance into heaven. Our rejection of him and a life lived in isolation from him leads to automatic rejection from heaven.

Returning to what Solomon has to say about Paul, Paul knows that death is nothing more than the test of life, the entry exam that judges not only a person's life here on earth but which also determines that person's future.

In understanding its purpose one would presume that Paul has discovered what he needs to do to pass this exam. This is something that is good practice and advice for each one of us.

A couple of weeks ago, whilst shopping with Sarah, I picked up a book called *Obituaries*.[4] As the name suggests, it is a book full of different people's obituaries. One day somebody is going to either write yours in the paper or speak it at your funeral. In all probability that person will not mention how you honestly faced death, but let's imagine that he or she did. Would he or she write about you as someone who faced death confidently, knowing what it was and where you were going? Or would he or she write about how in your last days you fell apart as you contemplated that which lay before you, not knowing where you were going or what was ahead?

Solomon asks, when it comes to death, how do you see it – as a dead end, or only as the end of the beginning?

---

[4] Hugh Massingberd (ed.), *The Daily Telegraph Book of Obituaries: A Celebration of Eccentric Lives* (Macmillan, 1995).

Conclusion

You and I have only one life to live. The question I want
to finish with is this: how are you going to spend it? Our
lives are not re-usable. We don't get another go.

If you're like me, you want the best possible ride through
life.

Could I encourage all of us to seek to be a Paul and not
a Ronald, to live with God in the frame and not with him
out of it. As Solomon has shown us, it is the way to live
and it is the best way to live.

Chapter 4A

God on ... a successful career

From 9 a.m. until 5 p.m., if you're lucky, every Monday through to Friday, for forty-seven weeks of the year, for between forty and fifty years of your life, you will work. In all probability your life will revolve around your job. People that you know best will be those that you work with. Who you are, how you describe yourself and how society values you will be determined by what you do for a living.

Some of you will hold down jobs that care for or offer a service to people, others will have jobs that pay well, others still jobs that interest them. In all probability the song of the Seven Dwarfs, 'Hi ho, hi ho, it's off to work we go', will not be the beat of your heart, but the rhythm of life means that you have to dance to that tune.

Since we will spend so much time in and at our jobs, I am sure you would agree that it is important that we ensure that to the best of our ability we get the most that we can from our work. As we all know, our jobs have the habit of taking the best from us – it is important therefore that we get the best from them.

In chapter 4 of Solomon's autobiography we find the author talking about the subject of work. Continuing his observation of life and his search for a life worth living, Solomon reflects on the working lives of several people that he has encountered.

Perhaps conscious of the amount of time that we spend at work, we find Solomon evaluating what he has seen, as well as noting his observations. Consequently, what we have in this part of his autobiography is a guide to a successful career; points worth pondering for those who want to get the best out of their jobs. One might suggest that what we have here is the first ever offer of in-service training for the ambitious worker.

What I want to do is look at what he has to say, the career guidance that he offers. OK then, so what does Solomon say makes for a good career?

Watch your motivation

In Britain there is a saying that you often hear when someone has just bought a new car or some other new possession. It usually comes as a judgement on and an excuse for the purchase. The saying is to do with the buyer's motivation. People say that the person is trying to 'keep up with the Joneses'.

What this means is that what the person has just bought was bought not necessarily because it was needed, but rather because the neighbours have one. Perhaps through envy, perhaps through covetousness, perhaps through an inferiority complex, some people strive to live at the same standard as their neighbours.

As Solomon observed the working habits of people, he noticed that this attitude was present in his day. He notes that many people work so that they might 'keep up with the Joneses':

And I saw that all labour and all achievement spring from man's envy of his neighbour.

Solomon goes on to say that, in his opinion, such a motivation to work is meaningless. He at this point does not justify his conclusion.

Perhaps Solomon had a nobler appreciation of work or was able to see the poverty of such a motivation. Perhaps he saw the dark consequences of such a motivation. We don't know. All we are told is that Solomon believes such a motivation to get out of bed and go to the office or the factory or the field, whether it is gloriously sunny or pouring down with rain, is not a good one.

The question we have to ask is, 'Is this our motivation?' Are we just looking to 'keep up with the Joneses'?

Guard yourself against laziness

Several years ago I came across a young man who had been very fortunate to be offered an apprenticeship with the British Steel Corporation. The particular apprenticeship that he won was something that was sought after by many of his contemporaries. The particular factory where he would work had a global reputation for the quality of training that it offered. Most of the people who were trained there had no problem getting a job elsewhere. The apprenticeships were in such demand that over 600 people had applied for the six places being offered that year.

Within a year of starting his apprenticeship the company asked him to resign. Although he had been given several chances, many encouragements and not a few warnings, the young man, although given a great opportunity, decided to be half-hearted about it. Some days he would not come to work, most days he would arrive late, almost every day he would lounge around, not listening, not learning and not working. From what I have heard since, life has not really picked up for this young man.

What Solomon records is that it will be the same for us if we don't heed his advice and guard against laziness. If you want to get the best out of your job, then learn this man's lesson – people who are lazy don't get on in work or in life.

As Solomon says:

> *The fool folds his hands and ruins himself.*

Know the place of contentment

Last week I met up with a friend of mine I hadn't seen for years. This person has really got on in life since I last saw him. Today he is the Managing Director of a growing company, has recently bought a nice house and has a lovely family.

What was particularly enjoyable about talking to my friend was that, within his success, he had still managed to keep a balance in life. I congratulated him on the fact that his company was doing so well. His response was, 'Yes, but you have to remember that there is an awful lot more to life than work. I enjoy working, it gives me what I need, but there are other things to life as well.'

If Solomon had been at that lunch he would have said a hearty 'Well done!' to my friend. As he says:

> *Better one handful with tranquillity than two handfuls with toil and chasing after the wind.*

This can be translated as 'Happy is the person who realises that work is not all that there is when it comes to life.'

It is important – yes. It enables us to live – yes! But it is not the place for the exercise of greed or workaholism or domination. It does have a part to play in our lives, but not the sole part.

What Solomon is saying is, when it comes to work, don't bite off more than you can chew. There is no need.

From the text above we can see that Solomon's motivation for these words is coming from a person he met who had sold out to the materialistic dream, given to take two handfuls of everything. Sadly, what that person discovered was a lot of toil and a lot of chasing after the wind.

How do we get the best from our jobs? By learning the importance of contentment.

As top dog, don't act as if you know it all

I was told recently of a Managing Director who was ousted by his company. The reason I got to hear about it was because one of my friends was the personnel officer who had to inform the mother company about his behaviour. Not an easy thing to do.

This Managing Director had been in office for some time. Unfortunately, during his leadership he had developed the habit of not listening to people. My friend reckoned that he had developed a deaf ear and a closed mind. The consequence was that at board meetings he didn't listen to the advice of others. It was reckoned that he had developed this attitude because with his promotions over the years he had developed a belief that he knew best.

Solomon says that when it comes to getting the best out of your job (particularly those of you who are top dogs) what you need to realise is that although you might be 'simply the best' this does not mean that you must, or can afford to, stop listening and learning from others. As Solomon says:

> *Better a poor but wise youth than an old but foolish king who no longer knows how to take a warning.*

Solomon says that remaining teachable is the secret of successful people at work.

Golden boys should appreciate the fickleness of popularity and the instability of power

Solomon says that we should remember that the people who are for us today could easily be against us tomorrow and that the company that is promoting us today could easily be the company that sacks us tomorrow. To paraphrase him:

> *I saw that all who lived and walked under the sun followed the 'golden boy', the boss's future successor. There was no end to all the people who liked him. But those who came later were not pleased with the man.*

When my boy started school, one of the children in his class had recently moved to the area because the boy's father had been headhunted by one of the local companies. This man had left a really good job and had done so with the assurance from his employers of good wages and great opportunities. Within a year of moving to the area, this man was unemployed. The company had been taken over and was changing the personnel. He had only been in post a short while and had been seen as one of the new golden boys of the company. Now he was out of work.

Solomon says that the person who has a true appreciation of his or her own popularity and power is happy and secure in him or herself. It will ensure he or she gets the best out of his or her job.

Conclusion

I recently went to a retirement party for a headmaster who had worked at a school for many years. He'd been there so long that today's pupils were children of those he had taught as children.

The head's retirement party was a great party. Not in the sense that everyone wanted to see him go, but that everyone really thought the world of him and were sad to see him leave.

As the man reflected on his time at the school and indeed in teaching it was obvious that, whether knowingly or unknowingly, he had taken Solomon's advice on how to get the best that you can from your job. This is God's advice for all of us. Consequently, he had had a very fulfilling career.

As Solomon stops in his journal to give us his insights, let me finish by encouraging all of us to heed his advice to ensure that we get the best that we can from our jobs.

Chapter 4B

God on ... friendships

The story is told of a stranger who on entering a new town asked a townsman whether it was a friendly town.

The townsman, who was known for his wisdom, asked the visitor if the last town that he had come from was a friendly town. The visitor answered that it was not. The townsman replied, 'Nor is this one.' With that the stranger left.

A little while later another stranger came to the same town and to the same townsman and asked this wise old man the same question: 'Is this a friendly town?'

Again the wise man asked the stranger whether the town that he had come from was a friendly town. The stranger answered that it was. 'Well,' said the townsman, 'so is this one.'

When it comes to making friendships, that old man knew that in most cases this is determined by whether or not there is an attitude of friendship in the person looking for new friends. That's why he asked the question that he did to those two travellers and why, in response to their answers, he gave the conclusions that he did about his town. To the one who had found his previous town difficult to make friendships in, the old man saw that this town would be similar. Yet to the man who had found his old town full of friendships, this old man said that this town would be just as friendly.

When it comes to friendship, Solomon is convinced that it is good to have friends. In his words:

Two are better than one.

However, Solomon is also aware of the many difficulties that people have in making and keeping friends. So, with that in mind, what he gives us are several reasons why we should be prepared to pay the cost of friendships, the price of adjustment, loss of independence, messiness, the sacrifice of time alone.

Mother Teresa once said that she believed that the greatest epidemic of the twentieth century was that of loneliness. Not leprosy or cancer, severe as they are, but rather the widespread isolation and sense of aloneness that many people today experience.

Solomon has just met such a dis-eased person:

There was a man all alone; he had neither son nor brother. There was no end to his toil, yet his eyes were not content with his wealth.

Suppose that this man is the top dog in his corporation. He is someone who in the world's eyes has become a career and financial success. All that we could want, this man has. Yet as Solomon talked to and looked at this man he saw that in the midst of his incredible affluence and success there was great loneliness. He had no one to share all that he had with, no one to leave it all to, no human being to give all that he was and had obtained.

To this man and to people like him Solomon addresses his words. This is wise advice to those who are loners or feeling lonely.

Friends can accomplish more together than apart

A couple of weeks back my family and I went on a holiday that one of our friends had organised. Although we were at the campsite for only a short period of time we had an absolutely great time. The food was excellent and the entertainment brilliant. There was a kids' programme for our children, which they thoroughly enjoyed. There were excellent facilities for swimming and playing tennis. So good was the camp that we and most of the people who were there are already looking forward to next year.

Now, as I have written, the camp was organised by my friend. The reason it turned out to be such a good camp, beyond his and most people's expectations, was that my friend took the advice of Solomon. Solomon says that two are better than one because when two work together the results are much better. My friend organised a great camp because he invited several of his friends to chip in and help him run it. Consequently, it became a team effort.

With friends working together the outcome surpassed the input. This is true in most of life's scenarios. Such, says Solomon, is a consequence of friendship:

Two are better than one, because they have a good return for their work.

If you fall down, a friend can help you back up

Many years ago I got myself into a difficult situation. As is often the case, I couldn't see it for what it was. Consequently, I began to suffer as an individual because of the circumstances I was in.

One day a friend of mine took me aside and had a long sober talk with me. He pointed out the mistake I was making and the terrible consequences that were not only beginning to happen but which would follow.

If my friend had not taken it upon himself to speak to me I wonder what sort of mess I would be in today. As it was, his advice saved me from another of life's potential ditches.

Solomon tells us that:

Two are better than one … if one falls down, his friend can help him up.

Thankfully, that was my experience.

To emphasise this point, Solomon also tells us how unfortunate it is therefore for the person who has no friends:

But pity the man who falls and has no one to help him up!

You have to wonder if that rich man that he had earlier met was on his mind when he wrote these words. He had fallen down. The particular hole that he had fallen into was the belief that what you have in your bank account and where you are in your job is more important than having a family and belonging to people. If only that man had had someone who could have stopped him from falling into that hole.

There is nothing wrong with having a good job or with being well off. What was wrong was that this person was not only in excess, but he had also contributed to the loss of that which was far more valuable.

Happy are those, suggests Solomon, who have someone like the Good Samaritan who will help them up when they fall down.

Friends can keep each other warm

I have a friend by the name of Mark. Mark is an incredible young man. At the moment Mark is attempting to be the youngest person to climb the highest mountain in each continent. With only a few left to climb it looks as if Mark is going to accomplish his goal.

The last mountain Mark conquered was Elbrus, which is the highest mountain in Europe. From the reports we have heard of the climb, this proved to be the most challenging yet. In fact, from what we have been told, Mark was lucky to come off the mountain alive. When he got to the top of the mountain he was found to be suffering from shock and hypothermia. Thankfully, though, a female climber from another party got into Mark's sleeping bag and used her body heat to help bolster his. They reckon that if she had not, Mark would have died.

Solomon says:

> if two lie down together, they will keep warm.

It is doubtful that Solomon had such a scenario as Mark's in his mind when he penned those words, but nevertheless Mark would be the first to testify to their truth.

In Chapter 3 we looked at Solomon's observations on how people view their lifetime, and what he concluded was that life is made up of seasons, which people could classify as good or bad.

When one is passing through a difficult season, that which aids one's journey is having someone to share it with. As someone once said, 'A problem shared is a problem halved.' Isn't it great when there is an operation to be faced or a difficulty in life to be overcome or simply endured to have someone to walk through it with? Such, says Solomon, is the consequence of friendship.

Two friends are more difficult to overcome than someone who is alone

As a teenager I supported Swansea City Football Club. As a keen follower, I went with some friends up to London to watch my team play West Ham.

Now, as a naive sixteen year old, I believed those who said that West Ham had the nastiest football supporters in the country, men who were continually looking to fight with the opposition. As such, you can imagine my delight then when my friends decided to travel up to the game by car and assured me that we would be able to park very close to the ground.

Unfortunately, our journey to London took far longer than we had expected; consequently, we realised that if we were ever going to get to the game then we needed to park the car on the outskirts of London and catch an underground train.

Never in my life have I been as frightened as I was travelling on that train across London. Why? Because not only was that the train which every West Ham supporter seemed to board to go to the game, but in going to support our team we had worn the team colours and were carrying our black and white scarves. It is surprising how difficult it is to hide a scarf when you don't want anyone to see it!

Solomon says:

Though one may be overpowered, two can defend themselves.

What this means is that there is safety in numbers. Admittedly, our numbers would normally have been enough for most situations, but when faced with a multitude of opposition supporters such was not the case. Nevertheless, what Solomon says is true: there is safety in numbers and strength to be found from being in a group, with other people. This is a further reason, says Solomon, why we should invest in friendships.

Conclusion

We have looked in this chapter at the characteristics of a good friend and the reasons for giving ourselves to developing such friendships. We have seen that friendship is a marvellous thing and that a true friend is a noble person. In concluding this chapter let me give you two encouragements.

Firstly, if in reading my words you feel that you could do with working on your friendships let me encourage you today to take one step towards friendship.

The second thing I want to note is this. As a Christian I have found that Jesus, the man who lived on earth some 2000 years ago, has proved himself again and again to be such a friend. He is the personification of all that Solomon has written about friendship. Why not develop a friendship with him?

During the course of his life Jesus was accused often by his opponents of being the friend of sinners and publicans. Such has been his willingness to befriend me that I would suggest he could do this for you too.

In regard to the friendship that Jesus gives, the writer of the hymn 'What a friend we have in Jesus' said it best.

Chapter 5

God on ... authentic spirituality

Imagine that you are at a Rugby World Cup final. The time is 4.20 p.m. The rugby this afternoon has been inspirational. Both teams have, on every possible occasion, attempted to run with the ball. The two scrum halves are vying for the 'man of the match' award. There have been five tries.

As the game draws near to the final whistle, the singing around the ground is growing in volume and passion. With but a few minutes to go Wales are beating New Zealand by one point. The Welsh fans, sensing that their team today has played with the spirits of men of long ago, of Barry John, of Gareth Edwards and Phil Bennett, of J.P.R. and J.J. Williams, are erupting with songs that express their patriotism, passion, excitement and respect. What these supporters are doing through their songs is attributing honour and worth to the team for its performance today. They see that the players have played like gods among men. If you listen carefully you can hear them sing:

> *Bread of Heaven*
> *Bread of Heaven*
> *Feed me now and ever more ...*

This action of attributing worth and honour to someone or something – worship would be the Bible's word – is what Solomon, the Old Testament king, writes about in the fifth chapter of his journal. This worship, however, is not that which you would find at a sports stadium or a pop concert or in a car showroom; rather it is the worship that you would find in the house of God. Solomon is talking about the worship of God. One could probably entitle this section 'What every worshipper of God should know'.

He asks, how do we approach the worship service? How should we come to church? What is the best disposition to take during the services? How will I get the most out of church? What is the relationship of Sunday morning to the rest of my week?

Now, at first sight such a topic as that of worship might seem out of place in the flow of the book. In the previous four chapters there has been very little talk about God, let alone worship, as Solomon has been looking at life under the sun – without God. As he has taken us to the workplace and the lecture theatre, the asylum and the playground, the bank and the shopping centre, Solomon has done so without God in the picture. However, here in chapter 5 he turns our focus quite unexpectedly by ninety degrees to talk to us about the worship of God.

With regard to why we find Solomon addressing this subject, the reasons are fourfold.

Firstly, because on the occasion that he did talk to us about God, what he had to say about him, particularly our relationship with him, necessitated further comment. This is that further comment.

Secondly, because Solomon wants people to have a spirituality that works. Solomon wants us to conduct a worshipful, meaningful and real relationship with God. What he tells us is what every worshipper of God should know. We live at a time when people are willing to believe in God but not to go to church. What we find happening in this passage is Solomon presenting such church unbelievers with a spirituality that should ensure church becoming relevant.

Thirdly, the reason why Solomon records for us the thoughts of God on worship is that he has gone and got a part-time job as a hypocrite buster. The Temple, the Jewish Temple that is, built by Solomon had over a period of time, had seen many people come to worship – the rich, the poor, people from all walks of life. As Solomon had watched them at worship he would have seen that which was true and that which was false. Solomon takes it upon himself here to remind us of what is important. Consequently, what we have here is the first ever 'good church guide'. If you are looking for a church to belong to, sick of ending up in religious buildings that God left a decade ago, then look to see if these characteristics are in place.

Fourthly, Solomon addresses the subject of authentic worship because he wants God to be pleased with what we bring to him.

Before we look at what Solomon tells us in his guide to good worship, I want within my introduction to say several general things about what he means by 'worship' in his chapter.

Firstly, in talking about worship it should be noted that Solomon is nowhere commenting on the Runcie debate – the style of worship. What he has to say is equally relevant to you whether you are an incense-swinging bells-and-smells lover or a hand-clapping flag-waver, whether you like choruses or hymns, silence or glass-shattering squeals.

Secondly, what we are talking about here is corporate worship, that which the church of God does together. We all know that worship is far more than what we do at church. The Bible teaches us that worship is also what we do at work and how we live our lives. Solomon's focus is on when those who are seeking God get together. In speaking about this he is addressing his thoughts to all those involved; both those who come to lead us and those who come to be led.

Thirdly, we should be aware that Solomon will concentrate his thoughts on the basics. The gist of what he will say to us is 'keep it simple'.

Fourthly, as we read these words we should sense that the spirit of them is to call us to excellence in worship.

As God speaks to us in these words, let's hear the call of the Spirit to come and live.

Get ready before coming to church

Guard your steps when you go to the house of God.

One of my most embarrassing moments happened several years ago at a Christian conference that is held every Easter, called Spring Harvest. To understand fully my embarrassing moment, you need to know that I was going at that time to a church where the preaching was, in my opinion, not the best. Some of the speakers could be described as unstructured. They would start a sermon at point A, then say something about point D, then go to point Z, then J, and then in the last two minutes attempt to weave a thread through them all and bring them together.

At those times when the speakers weren't too good, after the service some of the congregation would play a game to see how long each one lasted before getting lost. If someone suggested that he or she was still with a speaker after ten minutes, this claim was viewed with great suspicion.

Anyway, I was at Spring Harvest for the week with a
large group of people from the church I was worshipping at. One of the great things about Spring Harvest
is the bookstall that carries all the latest Christian
publications. It was there that I was embarrassed. You
see, whilst looking through the bookshop I discovered a
book entitled *101 Things to do During a Dull Sermon*.[5]
Thinking it would be a laugh, I had picked up a copy
with several other books to take back to our friends. Just
as I was about to go and pay, I bumped into one of the
speakers (probably the best of the lot) from our church,
who asked if he might see what I was buying. His question as to why I was buying that particular book still
haunts me.

What Solomon says is that the idea of preparing oneself for
boredom when going to church is an illustration of what it
means not to be one who is ready for authentic worship.
This is something that we are not supposed to do. That is
not what it means to 'guard your steps when you go to
the house of God'.

You see, 'to guard your step' means, if you want to offer
authentic worship, then make sure you have prepared
yourself to be alert and expectant for worship.

Many years ago I went on a Christian youth camp.
So strict was this camp that the leaders made all of us
dress up for services. Such, says Solomon, should be our
attitude, though for him it is not a matter of dressing up
fashionably, but mentally, physically and spiritually. If you
want to worship the Lord, then this, says Solomon, is how
you should come.

---

[5] Tim Sims with Martin Wroe and Adrian Reith, *101 Things to do
During a Dull Sermon* (Monarch, 1988).

'To guard your step' also relates to our attitude. Don't come thoughtlessly, carelessly, unaware of what you are doing. Don't be casual about it.

Consider your physical state. 'Don't come', says Solomon, 'to church as one who needs a nap, who has had such a busy and late night before that you are not in a physical state to receive, rather to sleep and dream. It will be impossible for you to concentrate. It's a turn off for the preacher to look out and see all these glazed expressions looking back, and it's a turn off to God as he comes to address and spend time with his people.'

What of your spiritual state? 'Don't', says Solomon, 'come as those who have wilful sins in their heart, as ones who are knowingly disobeying the Lord. In regard to others, don't whatever you do come as those who are at war with others, who are treating others differently from how they would treat the Lord Jesus by gossiping, backbiting, degrading character or bringing dissension. What you need to do is first go to that brother or sister you have wronged and be reconciled.'

What Solomon is saying is, when it comes to being a worshipper, don't be slipshod in your preparation.

For some people preparing for worship is not too difficult, but I know there is another side to it. There are others for whom the cycle of life is such that, whether through age, because of children or because of a partner's resistance to the faith, preparation of that sort is not possible.

For those who fall into that category, I think it fair to say that God understands and accepts. These words are for those for whom familiarity has bred contempt, people who, having an opportunity to prepare, don't. We all know what it is to argue with our partner before church or have our kids play up. If you are taking an

active part perhaps these problems are even more pertinent. It isn't our fault if the phone goes or the car won't
start.

What Solomon is saying is that through all of this you
should do your best to come prepared.

Although unseen by the human eye, there is outside your
church and most other churches a sign that says 'Danger
Zone'. It is a sign that informs us of the highly dangerous
activities that are taking place within the building – people
meeting with God.

To those in the know, Solomon says, 'Guard your
steps.'

Go near to listen

When I was at theological college, one of the lecture courses
that everyone had to take was entitled 'The Person of Christ
volumes 1–4', or 'PX1–4' as it was so affectionately abbre-
viated. The lecturer, who happened to be the principal of
the college, was an old man, who, because of his photo-
graphic memory, would simply recite the lecture from the
relevant chapters of his book.

Unfortunately, because of his age and his monotone
voice, students found nothing in the presentation of
the lectures to engage their attention. In fact, so badly
were they done that those who did attend would use the
occasion to write letters home, do any necessary revision,
or, if all was completed, count the number of tiles on the
ceiling, the number of people in the class or eye up one of
the other students. Listening to what was being said would
be the last thing on their minds.

Solomon says that when it comes to entering the house
of God our attitude should be completely the opposite,

regardless of the ability of the minister. When we come to worship we should come to listen.

It's an interesting point, isn't it, that worship, which we all associate with singing, is as much about being open to hearing as it is about expression. It was Henry David Thoreau who said that it takes two to speak – one to speak and one to listen. When we come to meet with God, we come to meet with one who is ready and eager to speak to us. What he looks for and what, according to Solomon, is an expression of authentic worship is an ear that is open to hear. Let me say that if we come to church with such an attitude we will find that God does speak to us. More often than not the reason we don't hear God speaking to us in church is because we did not come to listen.

Now, when Solomon says that we are to draw near and listen, we note that, although it is an encouragement to do just that, what he also means is that we are to do more than simply hear things. The Hebrew word for 'listen' carries with it the idea of understanding and obedience. We have heard, therefore, only when we have understood what is being said and when we have put what we have heard into practice.

What Solomon doesn't tell us, but which I think we should note, is that what we are to listen to is the Bible. A sacked priest was recently invited to take a seminar on the fact that he does not believe in God and how he feels that this is quite normal. The Bible tells us that we should not allow this sort of thing to be spoken of in church. We are to hear the word of God. The word of God is the written word, the Bible, the world's best-seller.

An old friend of mine says that one of the things that preachers can be guilty of is pointing out something to be done but not telling us how we can do it. How do we listen? How can we hear better?

Here are a few suggestions. We can pray and ask God to speak to us. We could cultivate a heart that is expectant – sure that God will speak to us. We can take notes and think in the week about what was said. At the end of the service we could spend a moment in quiet reflection.

Think before you speak

Many years ago my family and I joined some of our friends for a weekend away. The husband and I had planned to have a game of squash.

Now, I must be honest with you and say that I hadn't played squash for a long time, but, being into tennis at the time, I didn't think that I would have much of a problem with my opponent. In fact I reckoned that I would beat him with ease.

I was *destroyed*. He slaughtered me. It was so bad – it was almost un-Christian, the way he played! When we finished, our score reflected more an outside bet on a horse race than that of a squash match.

What made matters worse for me was that I had mentioned to some people, about ten to be exact, that I was going away for the weekend and that I was due to play this fellow. I had also told them what I expected to do to him. As it turned out my words were empty boasts.

The third thing that Solomon says in his brief guide to pleasing worship is that when we behave and talk like this to God we fail to give him the worship his name deserves. When it comes to worship there is no place for empty boasts. This Solomon labels false worship – acts of sin.

Solomon tells us not to offer the worship or sacrifice of fools.

As Solomon knew, there is scope for empty promises. At the end of the sermon or in response to an appeal we go forward indicating to God and to others that we are serious that on this point we will do what God has called us to. But we don't do it. We therefore act and speak before we have thought.

There is scope for empty prayers. We dishonour God, says Solomon, when we pray these grand prayers that have absolutely no meaning or sense to them; those prayers where we pray about everything but never ask for anything – prayers that are very much for show. In my opinion the strength of our prayers is seen by the degree of intimacy that is present in the prayer: not the number of scriptures, not the nature of the language, but the nature of the relationship.

There is scope for empty songs. In church we sing an awful lot of deep, meaningful words, words admittedly that are there to aid our worship. Unfortunately, according to Solomon, such words can also hinder our worship, for we can knowingly be seen to commit ourselves to things that are not true for us.

What makes these expressions of worship empty is that inwardly we know that we have no hope or intention of realising them. Also, we fail to appreciate what we are saying, and often speak and act with the wrong motives. When we do so we dishonour God.

What Solomon says is that we should not fall into such a trap, the trap of the fool, the fool who is quick with the mouth and hasty in the heart, the fool who has no reason to be such, for with God in heaven and us on earth, he is in a position to see all things.

What Jesus encourages us to do is to weigh up our intentions before we speak them.

The vows you have made – fulfil them

What is it about your partner that drives you up the wall? The thing that annoys my wife, probably more than anything else, is the fact that when I promise to do something I always promise to do it later and never now, and that usually it never gets done.

One particular vow that has got me into hot water a couple of times was my promise to check the level of the oil tank for our central heating. On the first occasion this happened we ran out of oil the day before my wife's birthday, and we had no heating that day and for most of her birthday. The second occasion was on the morning that we had a guest for lunch.

Strange, isn't it, that we husbands never learn?

The final thing Solomon says to us about authentic worship is that authentic worship occurs when one doesn't fail to fulfil one's vows.

Solomon says:

> *When you make a vow ... do not delay in fulfilling it.*

We need to realise that vows are not mandatory for the Christian. They are rather optional commitments or dedications that we take out with the Lord. Perhaps in response to an appeal, perhaps after some considerable thought on a given thing, we determine to do such and such an activity.

Solomon says that when we make such a vow we need to fulfil it if we are to be an authentic worshipper, someone who pleases God. We must not delay. None of this, 'Well, I'll do it next week or next month, or when I feel ready for it.' We must not evade it. None of this, 'I've changed my mind and I don't want to do it after all. I know I promised, but that was then and this is now, and right now I don't want to do it.'

We live in an age where people think that they can walk in and out of commitments. 'I know I said "I do", but that was then and this is now.' Our mentality is such that we think that the year-and-a-day law applies to God, if we let it lie long enough then it will be forgotten.

Within his diary Solomon gives us God's perspective and comments on such attitudes. He tells us that as far as God is concerned people who fail to fulfil their vows are fools. Indeed, in God's eyes it is better not to make a vow than to make one and then fail to fulfil it. What you need to do, says God, so that you don't find yourself in this predicament is ensure that your mouth does not lead you into sin. In the book of James, James likens the tongue to a spark that can set a whole forest on fire. God encourages us to master that flame. If we don't it will cost us. 'And by the way,' says God, 'don't take it out on the temple messenger [Amen to that!]. If you have promised something, and you wish to withdraw from that promise, don't get angry with my servant.

'In fact, if anything,' says God, 'you should be actively ensuring that you fulfil your vow, for failure to do so will cause me to be angry with you and punish you.' If you know the New Testament, you will know how true that was for Ananias and Sapphira, two people who made free will vows to God and then failed intentionally to fulfil them.

Let me ask you, are there vows today that you need to fulfil? Perhaps there are some within the family area? As husbands we promised to honour our wives and to love them. Are these vows being ignored? Are we so filling our time with other things that we are jeopardising that which we committed ourselves to before God? And what about our children? Are we giving them our time?

Conclusion

Let's bring this all together. We have seen in this chapter that Solomon's concern is that of worshipping God. We have seen that he is keen that such worship should be authentic, honest and true. Such worship is to be found when the basics are there: when people are preparing themselves to meet with God; when they come ready to listen to what God has to say; when what they say, what they do and who they are is authentic and not some hypocritical mask. True worship is found when they are working out their love vows to the Lord.

For some, these words might be like an un-climbable mountain, for others, excessive religious practice. 'I always thought they were fanatics, now I know!'

Solomon concludes his teaching on worship by high-lighting for us the key to climbing that mountain and the lens that puts such a supposedly fanatical scenario into perspective. He tells us that we are to stand in awe of God.

To stand in awe means to fear the Lord. Fear, in this context, means both a negative, paralysing grip and a liberating, right and respectful appreciation of the object of one's worship.

Fear of the Lord is, says the Bible, 'the beginning of wisdom'.

Chapter 6

God on ... the myth of money

'Stand and deliver! Your money or your life!' Those of you who have read about the notorious English highwayman Dick Turpin will know that this was one of his great sayings. It was his invitation to his unfortunate victims to either part with their wealth or lose their lives.

It might surprise you to read that this is also one of the Bible's great invitations. Although the Bible doesn't use those exact words, the sentiment of either hanging on to your wealth or saving your life is repeated throughout its pages. It should also be noted that in the Bible's declaration the personal benefit of such surrender is to the victim – that is, according to the Bible, if you surrender your wealth, you benefit.

Believing that money has for many become a replacement god for the one true God, the Bible invites us to give up our wealth, not that we might become financially poor, but so that we do not view it as something to be worshipped. As we stop focusing on wealth, we might turn our attention to God and become spiritually rich.

Now, as one can appreciate, surrendering one's wealth to another is no easy feat. Therefore, as Solomon issues this call, we also find him giving several reasons why we should wilfully give in. What we find Solomon doing in the second half of the fifth chapter of his autobiography is addressing and exposing the various myths that exist in regard to wealth, the folklore that has attached itself to money and elevated it to a place of worship in many people's lives.

He exposes four reasons. His purpose in addressing them is that we might readily surrender to God's highwayman.

The myth that money brings you satisfaction

A survey was published a while back on what young British people believed made for happiness. The report concluded that British teenagers put money above everything else. One of the comments in the findings read, 'The overriding discovery was the feeling that money was the doorway to modern life.'

This perspective is something that can be seen in recent book publications. Whereas once the theme of books used to be predominantly sex, more sex, affairs and then sex, they now concentrate on money, money and more money. People want to read about how others made their money, how they got their first deals, how they reached millionaire status. As one well-known pop group knew, the cry of many is 'Money, money, money'.

As I have indicated in earlier chapters, Solomon was someone who had amassed a great fortune for himself. Whether Solomon believed that money brings you satisfaction or not we do not know, but what we are told is that, having amassed great amounts of money, his personal experience was that at the end of the day it did not satisfy.

In fact, according to Solomon, the money that he had was one of the things making him dissatisfied. Why? Because in having it, it was creating in him a desire for more. As he says:

> *Whoever loves money never has money enough;*
> *Whoever loves wealth is never satisfied with his income.*

You know, I believe that money will never be able to satisfy us, not unless we evolve once more. Until:

> *We have developed four small wheels for our feet*
> *and a wire basket sprouting from our shoulders —*
> *until we have become shopping trolleys.*
> *For then and then alone will we be able to cry we are satisfied.*

(Source unknown)

The first myth that Solomon exposes is the one that would have us believe that money can bring satisfaction.

The myth that money solves all your problems

Many years ago the Pope went to Wales. At Cardiff, the crowd greeted him most enthusiastically, so much so that they sang him a song. They changed the words of a well-known Christian song, but instead of 'Our God reigns' they sang 'Our Pope reigns'.

Today another 'Pope' has come; one who would seek to lead us into many religious experiences. Just like the people in Wales, we too have greeted him most enthusiastically, so much so that we too have rewritten a song so that it is about him and that celebrates his all-powerfulness:

> *Nothing, nothing absolutely nothing, nothing is too*
> *difficult for you.*
> *Ah god money, thou hast made the heavens and the*
> *earth by thy great power.*
> *Ah god money, thou hast made the earth by thy*
> *outstretched hand.*
> *Nothing is too difficult for thee, nothing is too difficult*
> *for thee.*

Oh great and mighty money, great in counsel and
mighty in deed,
nothing, nothing, absolutely nothing, nothing is too
difficult for thee.

After all, money can buy you anything. Right?

It can bring you love. One bank suggested in its advertising that it could bring you love in the future:

Who's gonna love you when you are old and grey
Put a little love away.
Everybody needs a penny for a rainy day
put a little love away.

It can bring you spiritual blessing. Was it not Simon the Sorcerer who, seeing the great supernatural things that the Apostles were doing, attempted to buy his way into them?

It can take the waiting out of wanting. There is a story told of a woman who one day came to Jesus and reached out and touched him. For eighteen years she had been ill, for eighteen years she had sought out a cure for her illness. Being a woman of wealth she had used her money to try and buy healing. Unfortunately, it never made her better.

Someone once wrote that money can buy you all sorts of things, such as medicine, a house, food. However, it can't buy health, a home, an appetite. The writer ends by saying that although money can buy you a crucifix, it can't buy you a saviour; it can buy you a good life, but not eternal life.

Solomon says that such is the truth about money. It cannot solve all your problems. In fact, if the truth be told, it actually creates some of its own. What you find, says Solomon, is that when you have money you find that you get surrounded by a lot of people who want to take advantage of you. They say they are your friends, but you remember how they weren't there when you didn't have money.

Solomon says:

As goods increase, so do those who consume them.

The second myth Solomon exposes is that money can solve all your problems.

The myth that money gives you peace of mind

Billy Graham once described our age as the age of anxiety. His reason for such a classification was his opinion that never before have so many familiar props been removed from us. The removal of these props has caused us to be exposed to fear and uncertainty.

In the midst of such anxiety, many people believe that money is the way to experiencing peace. A former world boxing champion once said, 'Money quiets my nerves.' Many of us could say amen to such a statement.

Unfortunately, as many have experienced, mammon shalom is bankrupt. It might offer peace, but it will fail to deliver. You might be someone of great wealth, but if that wealth was achieved through dishonest gain then it is doubtful that you will ever be a person of peace. Those skeletons will be cause for serious concern. Should a newspaper take interest in your story then you can be assured of added anxiety. You can have more money than you will ever need. But will you have peace?

Solomon says that not only does money not give you peace, but it actually also adds to your dis-ease. It has the ability to hold sleep from you:

*The sleep of a labourer is sweet, whether he eats little or much,
but the abundance of a rich man permits him no sleep.*

Whether it is our lifestyle as a result of being rich or worry
over our money that makes us lose sleep, we cannot be
sure. It is probably both.

A doctor once asked his wealthy patient, 'What on earth
are you going to do with all your money?'

The patient replied, 'Just worry about it, I suppose.'

The doctor went on, 'Well, do you get much pleasure
out of it?'

'No,' responded the patient, 'but I get such terror when
I think of giving some of it away.'

As far as money and peace are concerned, Solomon tells
us that you just can't win.

One day, whilst talking to the people, Jesus brought up the
subject of worry. He noted that people worry about many
things: over what they should wear, over what they should
eat, about many issues. Having made this point, he then
asked the people why they worry. Jesus' perspective: the
reason that people worry is not because they do not have
enough money – as we have seen, money adds worries of
its own. The reason why people worry is because they do
not have peace with God. As he said, 'Look at the lilies in
the field and the birds of the air, they do not worry.' Why?
Because if God cares for them, how much more us.

The myth that money provides security

The story is told of two men who both decided to build a
house. One of the men, for reasons known only to himself,
decided to build his house on the sand; the other man
decided to build his on the rock. A little while after they
had finished their homes a severe storm broke out in their

area. There was torrential rain, followed by flash floods and high winds. It was a night of severe weather warnings. Unfortunately for the man who built his house on the sand, the storm proved to be too much for his foundations. His house collapsed.

The man who told that story told it to illustrate two things. Firstly, that when it comes to living one's life, and all that that involves – choosing a career, selecting a marriage partner, bringing up one's children and developing oneself – there is a choice of foundations that one can build upon; principles and truths that one can hold dear. We all have them – nobody believes nothing.

Secondly, the storyteller was keen to imply that although our society appreciates the variety of choices available to us, the suitability of most of them, if not all of them, bar one, is questionable. That one should build one's life on the rock is understandable; that one should build one's life on the sand is incomprehensible.

For most people, money is viewed as a solid foundation. A life built on anything other than that is seen as being unstable. After all, money makes the world go round. What Solomon says is that the truth is that money is the unstable foundation, for it will not give you security for this life or the life to come.

Not for this life, because you can quickly lose it. As Solomon says, wealth can be lost through some misfortune.

Not for the life to come, because it is not transferable into the currency of life on the other side. Solomon says:

> *Naked a man comes from his mother's womb,*
> *and as he comes, so he departs.*
> *He takes nothing from his labour that he can carry*
> *in his hand.*

Solomon tells us that money does not give us security.

Conclusion

To return to where I started this chapter, the great declaration of the highwayman was 'Stand and deliver! Your
money or your life.' If we have taken in what Solomon
teaches us about the true worth of money, we know how
to reply to the highwayman. Our best and wisest response
is to have such a loose grip on money that the struggle to
give it over is not so strong as to make you do something
stupid or life threatening.

But more than that, we must ensure that we never
accredit money with a worth that it does not deserve. It
is not and never will be God. Money is important and we
should be careful and wise in how we use it. However, we
should never give it divine powers.

As Jesus once said, no one can serve two masters:

*Either he will hate the one and love the other, or he will be
devoted to the one and despise the other. You cannot serve both
God and Money.*

The wise way to live is to appreciate the true worth of
money.

Chapter 7

God on ... how to be better off

How could you be better off? What, in your opinion, would lead to you having a better way of life?

In Britain, some people believe that they will have a better way of life by winning the National Lottery. From its logo to the way that it sells itself, Camelot realises that many people see that money and the winning of money is the key to a better way of life.

Some believe that they will be better off if they back the winner of a big horse race. A syndicate from a small Scottish town won £300,000, believing that such a win would lead to a better life.

Others believe that they will be better off if they live in an ideal home. Recently, a national newspaper sponsored an ideal home exhibition. Visitors to the show exceeded 500,000. Many of those present were there with the belief that simply improving where they live and what they live in will better their lives.

Still others believe that they will be better off by receiving acclaim. Many people dream of accomplishing something great, of doing something that no man or woman has done before: it might be in the family, it might be at work, it might be in the nation or in the world. All that matters is that in their 'world' they are given credit.

Again, others believe that they will have a better way of life by making a comeback. A little while back a well-known footballer was unable to play because of an injury he had picked up. If, during that period, you had asked him what could have made his life better, he would have told you that being able to play again was all he wanted.

Or again, some people believe that they will be better off by getting a better job. I know a guy who every week scours the jobs sections of the newspapers to see what is on offer. This man, unhappy in his present employment, believes that finding a better job will change things for the better.

Or yet again, some believe that they will be better off by keeping their health or getting back to full health. I heard recently about a woman's fight against breast cancer. A woman who lived life as carefree as one can, this lady commented on how the discovery of the lump threw her into a real tizzy. There are many people today who like her find themselves in what seems to be a long dark tunnel. What all of these people believe will make life better for them is to be made well.

Finally, some believe that they will be better off by being involved in a passionate relationship. Whether within or outside of marriage, whether casual or long term, whether affair or first-time romance, there are many people today who feel that this is the way to be better off. If you read the lonely heart columns or contact the dating agencies you will discover that there are scores of people who believe that this is what is missing.

There was a creative show called *Dilemmas* on British television recently. It was a programme that sought to test the morals of those on its panel and in its audience. The way the programme worked was by putting forward real-life scenarios and, as the story unfolded, asking people, at different points, to make judgements on how the people should act next.

In my opinion another name for the show could be *Wisdom*, for as well as testing one's morals, what the show also did was test one's wisdom. How on earth should that person act in that situation, what should he or she say, what should he or she do?

If one was to sum up what Solomon is saying in chapter 7 of his autobiography, a chapter that was written in the context of the question 'How can I be better off? – or, as he phrased it:

> *who knows what is good for a man in life?*

One would have to say that, as far as Solomon is concerned, such wisdom, which enables one to live life, to deal with difficult situations and to respond in each and every day of one's existence, is the ingredient that makes for a better life. Wisdom is defined by Solomon as a God-given ability to see life with rare objectivity, which enables a person to live through life with true stability.

Such is Solomon's wisdom and his belief in wisdom that what he does in his journal is to give us countless expressions of it. I mean, what is the point of saying, 'If you want a better life, get wise?' Surely it is wiser to say, 'You want a better life, let me show you what wisdom has done for me.' In an age like ours, which is more concerned with 'Does it work?' as opposed to 'Is it true?', such tact would be well received.

Before I look at what Solomon has to say about wisdom, let me first make several introductory remarks.

Firstly, it is important for us to realise that the person commenting is not one of life's all-time idiots. He is qualified to speak about his chosen subject. The words that are written in chapter 7 of Ecclesiastes are those of the man who is considered to have been the wisest man who has ever lived. What is more, if you read what he has to say in this chapter, you will also realise that they are words that he writes after having travelled far to observe their outworking and which he speaks having searched far and wide to see if there is any greater wisdom.

So I turned my mind to understand,
to investigate and to search out wisdom ...

Secondly, we must consider what point Solomon has reached in his spiritual journey. Most Old Testament scholars agree that he is at a turning point. In the story that Jesus tells about the prodigal son the son realises, after a period of high life and riotous living, that the only way ahead for him is to go back to his father's house. We could say that Solomon is at the stage of 'coming to his senses'. For the last six chapters he has been living in a world without God. What he is famous for, his wisdom, he has laid aside to indulge in the pleasures of the world. Here, in chapter 7, that all changes and the man begins to use again that God-given ability to see life with rare objectivity. As he does so you begin to see a change in his perception and in the direction of his life. Do note that he is not home, he isn't going to be home for some time, but he is turning to come home.

Thirdly, it is in the form of proverbs that Solomon chooses to communicate the wisdom that he has to give. Now, why he did that, I don't know. What we can be sure of is that it is viewed as a refreshing point in the book.

Most proverbs can be placed into one of three categories: contrastive, completive or comparative. In the first, two terms, referred to as a couplet, are separated by the word 'but' or 'nevertheless'. 'You can lead a horse to water but you cannot make him drink.' Completive proverbs link the couplet by 'and' or 'so'. 'A fool and his money ... ' The third type of proverb uses 'better/worse', 'than' or 'like'. Such comparative proverbs are often used by Jesus: 'The kingdom of heaven is like ... ' These are the proverbs we find in Solomon's journal.

Recently, an ancient stone slab was found in the north of Scotland. Some workmen renovating a young man's cottage came across it but, unsure of what it was, they decided simply to put it into the skip. Fortunately, the young man's father came to collect some of his belongings and saw the slab. Thinking it might be valuable he recovered it from the skip and made some investigations. His interest in the slab led to the eventual discovery of its historic worth and significance.

When one comes to Solomon's words in chapter 7 one can understand why at first glance many treat what they find here in the same way as the workmen treated the stone – they are unappreciative of its true value. 'This is a very puzzling passage of Scripture, with no obvious worth – best to simply skip it,' they think. However, as one investigates what is to be found, one will see that we have found something that is of significant worth, which answers one of today's most asked questions: 'How can I be better off?'

Wisdom will preserve us from taking wrong turns

What is your most embarrassing moment? One of my most embarrassing moments was when I tried to enter a car park by a very unusual route. I was visiting my friend in a small town in the south of England at the time and whilst he had gone off to work for the morning I decided to go and look around. The first problem I encountered was that I couldn't find a car park anywhere. The second problem was that when I did I couldn't find the entrance to it anywhere. I looked all around, but I couldn't see one. I knew that there had to be an entrance somewhere, but where could it be? I noticed at the side of the car park a small road with a dead-end sign. It seemed logical to me to believe that the entrance must be down there. As I drove down that road, I kept looking for the entrance sign, but there just wasn't one there. As I was nearing the end of the road, I saw what seemed to me to be a little hump from the road into the car park. That had to be it. It was a bit bad that they hadn't signposted it, but never mind, I had found it now. I was just about to drive into the car park when a bus driver flashed his lights at me. I didn't understand why at the time, but it was very kind of him to do that. When I started to come down the 'ramp' I discovered that I had in fact attempted to enter the car park via some steps. It's surprising how quickly a car park that was empty can suddenly be full of people, all looking at you.

What Solomon says is that wisdom enhances our lives, in that it preserves us from taking wrong turns on our journey through life, turns that cause us to end up in the car park of escapism instead of the multi-storey of realism.

This is particularly poignant, as we live in an age that is hungry for leisure and entertainment; we want to have the ability to fly from the Colditz of boredom and soar in the sensual and dine in the luxurious. Hollywood and such places make fortunes in expressing our thoughts for us. But, you know, it is actually better to live with the realities of life than to attempt to escape them. It is better, says Solomon:

to go to a house of mourning than to go to a house of feasting,
to go to the house of mourning than to the house of pleasure,
to be with the sad than the happy.

Not that there is anything wrong with feasting, pleasure and laughter, not at all, but rather that there is something better. Why is this 'something' better?

for death is the destiny of every man …

Wisdom, Solomon tells us, causes you to see this and therefore prepare yourself for it and then to live in the light of it. Wisdom causes you to be more concerned about your reputation than most anything else.

Wisdom provides us with a divine perspective

A little while ago a friend of mine was unjustly treated by an organisation that he and his family belonged to. Rather than make a fuss about the way they had been treated, he and his family withdrew their membership from the organisation.

If you had asked my friend why he had acted in this way, he would have told you that he had not withdrawn from the club because he was afraid of the people who were hurting him. Rather, he acted as he did for the good of those who would remain in it. His wider family had been members of that club for a long time and he knew how much they valued belonging to it. He also knew that if he caused a fuss, although in the right, it would cause a great deal of harm to his wider family. He decided therefore that walking away, although painful, was the best course of action.

I believe that my friend acted with a divine perspective. Rather than seeing things just from his own perspective, he was able to look at the issues from other people's points of view.

Wisdom, Solomon tells us, gives us that perspective, that ability to step above and beyond our own circumstances and look at an issue from a different angle. Solomon gives us three other examples of wisdom giving us a divine perspective.

The first example is in regard to the relationship between wealth and wisdom. Although it is possible to be rich and wise, at the end of the day it is far better to be wise than rich. How many people have had their political career cut short because of some financial scandal?

Solomon's second example concerns the place of submission or rebellion when one is going through a crisis. It is far better to submit than to rebel, for rebellion is pointless:

Who can straighten what he has made crooked?

When times are good, be happy. When times are not, don't rebel – consider how God has made the one as well as the other.

The third illustration of wisdom offering us a divine perspective is to do with our pursuit of character over inappropriate behaviour. At the end of the day, when all is said and done, it is better to die righteous than to live a long but sinful life. You see, what wisdom teaches us is that, from a divine perspective, a godly life is worth far more than a sinful life that is long.

Wisdom gives us balance

There is a saying that you can be too heavenly minded to be of any earthly use. However, that saying is actually wrong, because Christ was the most heavenly minded of people and was also of most earthly use. The sentiment in the verse, I think, is right, for there are people today who come across as so spiritual and holy that you wonder what on earth they have to offer.

What Solomon says is that true spirituality is not in over-righteous living, but rather in balanced living. Although you may look and act as if your head is in the clouds, your feet are firmly on the ground. Balanced living means having a lifestyle that is healthy and a spirituality that is honest.

Solomon says:

> *Do not be over-righteous, neither be overwise —*
> *why destroy yourself? ...*
> *It is good to grasp the one*
> *and not let go of the other.*
> *The man who fears God will avoid all extremes.*

Wisdom gives us strength

When you look at people who are in a leadership position, what do you see? When you look at a church minister, or a manager, or a president, what do you see?

In regard to a minister, some people reckon that a pastor is six days invisible and one day incomprehensible. But, seriously, what do you see? When I look at people in leadership I see people who are desperately trying to do their best, but often failing to do so. I see men and women who are continually trying to please everyone, but often failing to please anyone. Sadly, I sometimes see people who are using their position for their own ends.

What Solomon says is that wisdom gives the strength to cope with such contradictions, in life and in a leader's life.

> *Wisdom makes one wise man more powerful than*
> *ten rulers in a city.*

The way that it does this is by giving us a realistic appreciation of the people who lead, and in so doing it prepares us, hence strengthens us, for the occasions when they live up to the worst of our expectations.

As Solomon writes:

> *There is not a righteous man on earth*
> *who does what is right and never sins.*

I have been in many churches where people in leadership have failed and where members of the church have been devastated by what has gone on. We cannot excuse or overlook failure, but what we can do is to see it for what, at the end of the day, it really is: human beings with the divine still having much to do in their lives.

But, you know, it is not just in the area of coping with leadership failure that wisdom gives us strength. What wisdom also does is give us strength to avoid the pitfalls of gullibility and of returning criticism.

As it is written:

> *Do not pay attention to every word people say,*
> *or you may hear your servant cursing you –*
> *for you know in your heart*
> *that many times you yourselves have cursed others.*

Wisdom gives us insight

Many years ago when Billy Graham was starting out as an evangelist he held a meeting with members of his team to talk about the guidelines that were to determine their behaviour as they engaged in their work.

Perhaps aware that so many people had lost their way in the type of work that he was engaging in through inappropriate behaviour, perhaps determined that he should not become another statistic, he set about detailing how he and his team were to live.

Solomon says that the reason that wisdom makes us better off is that it gives us the type of insight that Billy Graham and his team had – the insight to see that there are many pitfalls in the type of work that they were doing and that if they were to avoid them then they needed to prepare for them.

So keen is Solomon to encourage us to see the insight that wisdom gives that he tells us of an occasion when it helped him. On his journey he came across a woman who enthralled him, who enticed him. What he discovered because of the insight that wisdom gave him was that she was in fact a snare.

If you had talked to British Prime Minister John Major during his term of office he would have told you that this sort of wisdom was just what his party needed. This was not just because the Conservative Party needed to figure out how on earth it should respond to the poor show it had in the Scottish elections, or what it should do about the Spaniards' fishing claims. It was rather because of all the chaos and bad publicity the party had endured over the previous months due to sexual misconduct by its members. People spoke of the 'Hall of Shame', a hall full of individuals who were in desperate need of the insight that wisdom gives but who tragically fell because of the lack of it.

Conclusion

As I conclude this chapter, the question that I want to ask is this: 'How do we get this wisdom?' If there are so many benefits of being wise, how on earth can any of us live without it?

Well, the answer is found in part in Solomon's journal and in part in a book in the New Testament. From the journal we see that wisdom is not a commodity that can be got from earthly activity, for indeed it is not of earthly origin.

> *'I am determined to be wise' –*
> *but this was beyond me.*
> *Whatever wisdom may be,*
> *it is far off and most profound –*
> *who can discover it?*

But we should not lose heart because of that, for such wisdom can be found. James, the brother of Jesus, tells us in his letter that it is to be found in God and is available for the asking.

> *If any of you lacks wisdom, he should ask God, who gives generously to all without finding fault, and it will be given to him.*

I invite you to ask God to give you that wisdom.

Chapter 8

God on ... the qualities of a good boss

What, in your opinion, makes someone a good boss? If you were a prospective employee, what type of person would you like to work for? If you are a boss, what type of leader are you trying to be? If you are a human resources director, what type of bosses would you say are the most employable?

Many people in business believe that a good boss is someone who is able to optimise his or her use of time. Efficiency is the way to move up the corporate ladder. Be as efficient as you can. Give the best that you can and maximise your potential. Order your day; prioritise.

Some think that a good boss is someone who can motivate others. One needs to have the ability to empower others with dreams and visions, to cause others to see their significant role in the overall scheme.

For others, a good boss is best defined as a team player. 'Synergy', they call it, the creative energy that emerges when colleagues test out concepts and ideas in creative discussion. Part of this is also working as a team. Leadership is team orientated.

Again, others would say that a good boss is someone who is psychologically aware. It's all about self-esteem. If you can cause your people to feel good about themselves, about what they do and about how they are doing it, then you are going to lead a very productive company. What you need to do, therefore, is to discern what it is that will release such pride in your workforce.

Those who have worked hard to get where they are would understand being a good boss in terms of sacrifice. It's all about putting in the hours. If you want to get on in the world, then you gain through pain.

For some, a good boss is defined by his or her golf handicap.

In chapter 8 of his autobiography Solomon gives us his answer to the question 'How can I be a better boss?' Continuing his theme of wisdom and wanting to flesh it out some more for his readers, he paints for them a picture of the consequences of being a wise person in leadership. What we have here, therefore, are the words of the Old Testament business guru, a man skilled and knowledge-able in leadership and the developing of it.

Before we look at what Solomon has to say about being a good leader, let me first make some introductory remarks.

The first is a general remark about the type of leader that we are thinking about in this chapter. We are, I am told, going through a transition in the type of leaders that are emerging and that are needed. It seems that we are moving away from the transactional leader and towards the transformational leader. Transactional leaders are leaders, more correctly termed managers, who seek to work with what they have; transformational leaders are those who seek to change what they have for the better. The qualities that Solomon identifies for us are central to those that his headhunters would be looking for in transformational leaders.

Secondly, we need to be aware that the particular context that Solomon has in mind as he speaks about how to be a better leader is that of the king and his servants. However, we should also be aware that the principles set out here are transferable to any person who has authority over others. What Solomon has to say, therefore, from his seminar notes on developing effective leaders can be applied to parents in the home as they rear children, managers in small or large businesses and even leaders in the church.

Thirdly, in addition to focusing in on good leaders, we should note that Solomon also takes time to talk about good followers. Perhaps Solomon had discovered that good leadership is not just about the person in front but also those who are following. With regard to the qualities of good followers Solomon lists four. They are:

Obedience:

> *Obey the king's command ...*

Commitment and stickability:

> *Do not be in a hurry to leave the king's presence ...*

Integrity:

> *Do not stand up for a bad cause ...*

Respect:

> *a king's word is supreme ...*

My last observation, before we look at what Solomon has to say to us, is that who we are as people is of greater importance than how we manage or what we manage.

So let us look to see what this Old Testament king, who would grace any leadership position, has to say about the qualities of a good boss. For simplicity's sake I have grouped what he has to say under four headings: the qualities of a good boss in regard to his or her mind, heart, spirit and actions.

The mind of a good boss

Several years ago when I became the leader of a local church I arranged to have my leadership style measured on the 'team management wheel'. This 'wheel' was a set of questions that identified the particular strengths and weaknesses that I had as a leader.

My reason for doing this was to gain greater insight into how I lead, how I work with others, how I process information and the preferred roles that I have within the team. Having identified my preferences, the company that conducted the tests was able to identify that I was primarily a thruster organiser.

It was obviously an accurate assessment, because when the personality profile, the result of the questions I had answered, came back to me, all my wife did for an hour was laugh at how well they knew me.

Anyway, the reason I mention the team management wheel is that, from my understanding of it, there doesn't seem to be a right or a wrong way to lead, simply various preferences that one could have in leadership. You could be this or you could be that.

As Solomon opens up the subject of leadership what he identifies is that the qualities he mentions are not options but necessities for any would-be leader.

You must, says Solomon, have a clear mind. You must
be someone who is able to see below the surface of things,
the foundation, to see the picture behind the blurred image,
to understand the whole picture, to understand the deeper
meaning of things. 'Why?' is a question you must always
be asking. We get that from Solomon's use of the Hebrew
word for 'interpretation', which carries with it the meaning
of 'see through the mystery of something'.

Solomon also says that, in addition to clarity, a good
mind is characterised by keen judgement. One thing that
is sometimes true of managers is that many of them have
been promoted too far up the ladder, to the level, usually,
of incompetence. They find themselves in leadership roles
that are beyond them. Solomon says that a good leader is
someone who (within his or her level of management) has
keen judgement. What he means by that he spells out for
us. They must be people with good timing and who can
discern the right course of action:

> the wise heart will know the proper time and procedure.

What Solomon also says, and all of us who are in leadership
or management will know that this is true, is that often
such thinking and intuitive reacting is done while under
considerable pressure.

A leader who exhibited these qualities was a man called
Nehemiah, who lived in the fifth century BC. The context
within which Nehemiah expressed these qualities was
his reaction to the looting and destruction of his home
city of Jerusalem and his attempts to bring about an end
to this.

Nehemiah was a Jew. The Jews around that time had
been overrun by the Babylonians and then taken over
by the Persians. During the invasion the city had been

brought to ruins, but over a period of time the adminis-
tration became slightly more lenient and allowed a few
Jews to return. Although noble in their attempts to restore
the city, the returned exiles were continually defeated due
to the activities of a group of Government appointees who,
having an axe to grind against the Jews, did everything
within their power to keep the city in ruins, both physically
and economically.

History tells us that Nehemiah took it upon himself to
right this situation. The way that he exhibits the qualities
that Solomon says make for a good boss can be seen in
how he came to understand the situation, in how he came
up with the right procedures to rectify things and how he
got his timing right.

How did he come to understand the situation correctly?
By discovering why these local Government officials were
against the city; trying to understand why the king was
allowing this behaviour, grasping why the people were
unable to defend themselves against such attacks and, on
a deeper and more religious level, discerning why God
had allowed this to happen.

Figuring out the best way forward was through a
focused time of contemplating the issue and then bringing
the king into the situation.

Nehemiah's wisdom was again exhibited in the way
he dealt with the various complex issues that confronted
him when he got to Jerusalem. How should he work out
his programme of making the city physically safe? How
should he ward off the dangerous officials? How should
he draw the people together? How and when should he
launch his building and restoration programme? How did
he get the people to carry on working when the officials
sought to stop the work, seemingly legally, then deceitfully,
then with physical violence?

Solomon tells us that a good leader is someone with a clear mind and keen judgement. Nehemiah illustrates that truth well. If you and I are to be good leaders then the same must be said of us.

The heart of a good boss

Some time ago, a top American executive search firm conducted a survey of CEOs of the top one hundred companies in the New York area to find out what character traits were valued most by leaders. The firm was interested in what traits junior executives should cultivate in themselves in order to become the kind of corporate leaders who would be deemed most desirable. While honesty and fairness ranked highest, there were other important character traits that were cited. The advice of these top CEOs went like this.

Never compromise on matters of principle nor standards of excellence, even on minor issues.

Be persistent and never give up.

Have a vision of where you are going and communicate it often.

Know what you stand for, set high standards, and don't be afraid to take on tough problems despite the risk.

Spend less time managing and more time leading. Lead by example.

Bring out the best in people. Hire the best people you can find, then delegate authority and responsibility. Stay in touch.

Accept blame for failure and credit others with success.

From the responses given, the company that sponsored the survey concluded that what was being advocated more than anything else were character traits and values that come from a religious source. In reading what Solomon says, it seems he would say a hearty amen.

In Solomon's view, a good boss is one who is humble, someone who has a true perspective of him or herself, a perspective within which he or she does not see him or herself as being as capable as God, and therefore does not act as if he or she were God's gift to the corporation. However, a good boss also appreciates that God has given him or her certain abilities which he or she can contribute to the company.

Now, what is blatantly obvious is that this cuts across many leaders' views today. Many people believe that if they are going to get on in the world then they will do so through power – power dressing, power lunches, power image. They imagine that it is through force that one gets to the top. Solomon says that power is not what makes you a good leader, rather it is a realistic perspective of the scene and a consequential disposition.

> *You can't read the future, so why be so sure?*

> *You can't really change people, so why be so confident?*

> *You don't know it all, no one can, so why act that way?*

In addition to having a humble heart, Solomon says that a leader's heart should also be joyful.

Several years ago an American sociologist wrote a book entitled *The Kingdom of God is a Party*.[6] It was an attempt

---

[6] Tony Campolo, *The Kingdom of God is a Party* (Word, 1992).

on his part to bring a more biblical perspective to work, to the family and to life. Acknowledging that Christ came to make life more like the fairground than the cemetery, the author believed that boredom and drudgery had become the norm.

Solomon says that a good manager is someone who is caught up in restoring joy to the workplace. This is a joyfulness that shows on his or her face and therefore is a joyfulness that he or she has given out to others.

> *Wisdom brightens a man's face*
> *and changes its hard appearance.*

This joyfulness is something that he or she has incorporated into all of his or her life and which comes from having a godly perspective on life.

The spirit of a good boss

A little while ago, a friend of mine went along to a promotional meeting for a new men's organisation that hoped to set up a group in our town. It was interesting that one of the things the group communicated during the evening was its perspective on the priorities of life. It went something like this:

> *Family first.*
> *Job second.*
> *Commitment to the organisation third.*

From what Solomon tells us about good bosses we can suggest that these men have not fully grasped the whole picture. This lack of vision is also something of which Christians are sadly guilty.

What they have not grasped is that there is a spiritual part to life. This is something that many people are beginning to become aware of in secular life in general and in the management world in particular. The new age movement, for instance, is finding a very receptive audience in this arena. This spiritual aspect makes us better and more fulfilled people. Many management theorists now talk of a leader's 'SQ' – spiritual quotient.

People have begun to departmentalise their lives. There is the family, there is work and there is the organisation. For religious folk it is God, family, work and then church.

Solomon does not take it that way; in fact he takes it for granted that God is part of every aspect of our lives. What we do in the office is as much to do with our relationship to God as to anything else. As far as Solomon is concerned, there is no division. One of the things that all of us have to grasp, whether it be as a leader or as workers, is that work is as much sacred as is going to church. What we do with our hands or with our minds or in our 9 a.m. to 5 p.m. or 9 a.m. to 8 p.m. jobs is as worshipful as what we do when we come to church. One's calling to the directorship is equal to another's calling to the ministry. In God's eyes they are all service and they are all related to him.

Since that is the case, there is need to have a spiritual dynamic in one's life and that dynamic must work out in one's work life. What Solomon tells us in this short section on being the best leader you can be is what characteristics one should have in one's spiritual life.

We know some people get where they do because they lie and cheat, because they push and scream. Solomon says that a good leader is one who is conscious of the fact that he or she is where he or she is because that is where

God wants him or her to be. There is no place for sibling rivalry like that between Esau and Jacob over their father's estate. There was no place for Joseph's brothers to do the things that they did to him to prevent him from reaching the position of master.

The realisation that you are where God wants you to be gives tremendous strength and confidence. One of Jesus' biographers comments on how from such a position of knowledge he was able to serve so well. The reason was that his service did not threaten his self-worth.

In addition to being called of God, Solomon says that a good leader is also someone who has the fear of God within his or her spirit.

Within many companies there is often a method of appraising people, of measuring and reporting on how they are doing or not doing. To some extent this is a form of accountability. What Solomon says is that a similar system is in operation with God. Each of us will give an account before God of how we have acted; how we have lived and what we have been; what we have done and what we have become. Although in infancy, this thought is expressed in Solomon's words:

> *I know that it will go better with God-fearing men,*
>   *who are reverent before God.*

This sense of judgement and accountability is expanded in the New Testament.

The wise boss, says Solomon, is someone who lives in the light of such accountability. What is more, such accountability will:

> *save him or her from acting wickedly during difficult times.*

> *save him or her from bringing harm on him or herself.*

> *ensure a commitment to character more than results.*

It was Martin Luther who spoke those memorable words 'Here I stand, I can do no other' as he faced the weight of the Catholic Church, as he faced rejection and possible death. Yet what could he do when there was no way out for him? Called of God, with the fear of God, how else could he respond?

Solomon tells us that good leaders sense a call from God and know the fear of God.

The actions of a good boss

Since leadership involves interacting with people and the leading of people, in their relationship with these people good leaders are those who have discreet mouths and also exercise discipline.

They should say only that which should be said, to whom it should be said and when it should be said. This is more implicit in the text than explicit. Since the king's word is as authoritative as it is, it is important that he uses it rightfully. Power playing or mischievous gossip or rumour mongering are out of place in the leader.

Several years ago, when one of the churches I worked with had a mission team, I talked to the leader of the team about the team dynamics and about how I felt each member was doing. Within a day the rest of the team knew what I thought and what I did not think. Such behaviour on the part of the mission team leader was unacceptable.

Concerning exercising discipline, coming back to Nehemiah, his story is one of both success and tragic failure because of the presence of discipline and the lack of discipline.

One of the reasons that it was a success was that Nehemiah was a man who dealt properly, fairly, biblically with those who needed to be disciplined. We see such discipline going on in his dealing with Sanballat, Tobiah and Geshem the Arab, the corrupt Government officials. We see it in the way that he dealt with the nobles, the rich folk in his volunteer movement who, during a time of poverty, were lording it financially over those not so fortunate.

The reason that the story of Nehemiah is one of tragic failure is that the discipline that should have existed didn't. Sanballat, it seems, had friends in the centre of Nehemiah's work team. That problem was never dealt with, which meant that, fourteen years later, when Nehemiah returned to Jerusalem, he discovered that although the walls were up his other task of building up the spiritual life of the people had not been carried through. Did he know about that relationship link? If he did, it was one of his greatest mistakes; if he didn't, what a tragedy to have missed it.

Solomon tells us that we should discipline and discipline quickly where it is needed. It is a mark of a wise leader.

Conclusion

In his book *Issues Facing Christians Today*[7] John Stott notes how in our world we are facing a leadership crisis. Our world is at a crucial stage. There are problems on a global scale that need to be addressed, problems such as the nuclear bomb, human rights, environmental issues, economic difficulties. There are problems with the family, in the community and in the workplace. There are problems and difficulties in the only divine institution that can possibly help humankind – the church.

---

[7] John R. W. Stott, *Issues Facing Christians Today* (Marshall Pickering, 1990).

What is needed now more than at any other time are leaders, true leaders, transformational leaders, leaders of the calibre that we have been looking at in this chapter. We need people with minds that God has made wise, hearts that he has readied, spirits that he has prepared and who will honour him with wise living and leading.

The challenge before all of us is to stir ourselves to being that type of leader.

Chapter 9

God on … life – a guide to living

When you look in the mirror, what is it that you see? This morning, if you managed to glance in the mirror, who was it that you encountered?

When I look in the mirror I see a mixture of the following.

A man. (I might add that that is not what my boy sees – he says I'm a wuss and a fat man.) A man who, like other men, has temptations that he needs to keep a check on, character traits that he needs to develop and a phobia of 'going to the doctor's' which he has to ensure does not get in the way when he really is ill. A man who, when he says 'I'll do it in a minute', needs to realise that a minute is sixty seconds and not sixty minutes or days.

A father of two children. The father of a boy who seems to exhibit everything that is good about his mother and me. He is intelligent, good looking, an athlete, with good social skills and a great sense of humour (and he obviously gets one or two things from his mother). The father of a wonderful girl who once suffered from one of those childhood illnesses, 'can't hear'. Whenever her mother or I asked her to do something that she did not want to do she couldn't hear.

A husband, of Sarah, who loves him dearly and who is still his best friend. Sarah said that I'm not allowed to say any more.

A son. A son who recently had to do a very difficult thing. For several years my mother has been under observation for cancer. She had surgery to remove a tumour in 1995. A little while ago, I spoke to her specialist, who told me that she now has only a few months to live. Unfortunately, she had not taken in his comments about the seriousness of her condition. Last Monday I went to see her and to tell her that she is going to die.

A brother. One of the reasons that it was decided that I would talk to my mum is that my sister had got it into her head that the doctor did not want my mother to be aware of her situation.

A grandson, who must continually keep an eye on his gran. This lady is very important to me in that she brought me up and still tries to keep her eye on me. Having nearly lost her through ill health these last two winters, she is a constant thought on my mind.

The owner of a dog called Holly. A dog who has come to understand her place in the family, but who continually seeks to exert her authority over me. At a recent dog obedience class, Holly came last but one.

A Christian minister. I not only believe in God and enjoy being his child, but I have (as we all do) the great privilege of being able to spend all of my time working for God. I get invited to go to places and talk about Christianity. I run a faith charity that gets up to all sorts of exciting things.

Me. I see someone who is thirty-nine years of age. A Welshman who loves life and is enjoying it, yet who is having to deal with lots of very difficult situations. I see someone I like.

Now, as I asked at the beginning of this chapter, when you look in the mirror, what is it that you see?

In chapter 9 of Solomon's autobiography, he tells us about what he sees when he looks into the mirror of life. I would like to make some suggestions about what all of us should see. I want to look with you at what he has to say about life; to look at what the Bible says about life and its guide to living. We shall look at what the Bible sees as the realities of life, how we should act in the midst of these realities and what guides our actions.

Now, as we look at what Solomon has recorded about life and the living of it, let us remember that Solomon was someone who was well qualified to make these comments and also that he speaks from two viewpoints. He speaks as one who sees things from under heaven and as one who sees things from under the sun.

What are the realities of life?

In the 1966 World Cup final England beat Germany 4–2. The thing that determined the difference between the two countries was a goal scored by Geoff Hurst. From that day to this, that goal has been discussed, not because of the quality of play that led up to it, nor because of the power or distance from which it was struck, but rather because of the dispute that rages over whether or not it went over the line. Try as they might, with computer-enhanced projections and tracking, with the film from cameras stationed at various points, the question that is still asked is, 'What's the truth about that goal? Did it go in or did it not?'

It's the question of truth that Solomon is concerned with as he pens these notes on the realities of life. In the previous chapters Solomon has torn away the myths of life. In the first eight chapters of his book he has exploded various world-views: materialism – that you are what you own and where you shop; epicureanism – that a fix a day would help you work, rest and play; humanism – that the future of humanity rests with us and that we need to find the god within us; fatalism – that life is nothing more than being dealt 'chance cards' and doing the best you can. In these notes Solomon gives us that which is left.

Firstly, we are all going to die. The great statistic of life is that one out of one people die. John Betjeman once asked why people waste time coming up with 'dainty names' for death. Perhaps they hope to ease us of its reality, for the truth is that it is the one true fact of life. Have you ever gone passed a cemetery and said to the person you are with, 'Do you know how many people are dead in that cemetery?' The answer is 'All of them!'

For Solomon, death is an often-paddled stream. We are given by Solomon four features of this reality.

It will happen at an unknown hour. You can be helping your mum in the kitchen and slip and fall on a knife, or you could be waiting for a bus and have a heart attack.

It awaits us all. Whatever our theology, whether it be that of Billy Graham, the Pope, a Hare Krishna or an atheist, whatever our morals, whether Mother Teresa or Madonna, we will all die.

It is unavoidable. As Oscar Wilde once said, we can escape almost anything these days, but we still can't escape death.

For those under the sun, the reality of death is a horrible thing, because there is seemingly nothing afterwards. A couple of years ago I had a dream where I woke to find myself in my own coffin being rolled into a crematorium's furnace. Despite the fact that I cried and cried for help, no one could hear me – they were all singing. I awoke from my dream just as the flames were beginning to come into the coffin. Such is the reality for those who die outside the Christian faith.

Secondly, uncertainty awaits us all. Sometimes you can feel that life is like a game of Russian roulette, nothing but chance.

We don't know whether we will be loved or hated, accepted or rejected. When we were living in Scotland, Glasgow Rangers bought Paul Gascoigne. You know, the papers were full of speculation as to whether Paul would be accepted by the Rangers fans or, as many suspected, rejected; whether he was going to get the kiss of greeting or the Glasgow kiss (a head-butt). Such, says Solomon, are the uncertainties of life.

Such are life's uncertainties that you don't get the results you expect. Solomon lists for us five qualities for success, those that you would expect to find in any 'do-it-your-self' success book, or in any seminar on how to become a winner. The expectation is that those who are swift, strong, wise, brilliant and learned will get on in the world. What Solomon suggests is that that is not always the case.

> *The race is not to the swift*
> *or the battle to the strong,*
> *nor does food come to the wise*
> *or wealth to the brilliant*
> *or favour to the learned;*
> *but time and chance happen to them all.*

Thirdly, evil and insanity reside in the human heart. A friend of mine works in the head office of a large company. A little while ago he told me about all that was going on in his place of work. To say the least it was incredible. It seems that at his office at the moment there is nothing but affairs. The boss is having an affair with his secretary, one of the other directors has just started an affair with one of the employee's wives, and one or two other people had recently been discovered to be having long-term extra-marital relationships with other workers.

My friend's opinion is that these people must be crazy. They do not consider all they could lose for a quick, usually mid-life-crisis induced, thrill: a wife, a home, their children, the respect of others and even their own self-respect.

Solomon says they are out of their minds. You see, one of the things that people are prone to every now and then is losing their mind. It happened to the man in one of Jesus' stories – the prodigal son; it has happened to countless others down the ages. Such, comments Solomon, is the reality of life: that our world is filled at times with insanity.

Furthermore (and unfortunately), says Solomon, you can get caught and affected by others' insanity:

> *As fish are caught in a cruel net,*
> *or birds are taken in a snare,*
> *so men are trapped by evil times*
> *that fall unexpectedly upon them.*

Through no fault of your own, like those who are knocked down and killed by reckless drivers, you can become a victim of this evil insanity.

Finally, there is hope for the living. It is not all doom and gloom. In the joyful words of the British lottery, 'It could be you.' You could win a fortune. As Solomon says, in a well-known proverb:

even a live dog is better off than a dead lion!

Why? Because when you are alive you can prepare yourself for death. Because the very fact that you are alive means that you can live. Sure, there might be some harsh realities to life, but take comfort, for even with the storms of life there is still a rainbow with the possibility of that pot of gold.

Those of you who have read the biblical story of Jacob will realise that it is just such a tale. Jacob was a man who throughout the course of his life endured an incredible amount of suffering. He went through a famine, the rape of his daughter, rejection by his family and the supposed death of Joseph. Yet in the midst of all that there was hope – Benjamin, who was a replacement for Joseph; food in Egypt; reconciliation with his brother; the opportunity to bless Pharaoh; the discovery that Joseph was alive.

What's the truth about that England goal? Did England score or not? Nobody knows. In all probability we never will. What's the truth about life? That there are to it several, indisputable realities.

What should be our disposition in life?

If these are the realities of life, how, oh how, should we live through life? Solomon's answer, in the words of the well-known, but possibly irreverent, Monty Python song, is that we should always look on the bright side.

I am one of those closet Trekkies. In the words of Spock to Jim, we should be those who are 'enjoying the journey'.

I don't know if you have seen the film *The Great Escape*, which stars Steve McQueen. The film is all about the British attempts during the Second World War to break out of a German prisoner of war camp. At the end of the film, the closing sequence has several recaps of incidents featuring McQueen. Each of them concludes with him, despite the difficulty that he is in, smiling.

Such shots, says Solomon, are to be our disposition through life, our postcards on life.

In fact, Solomon is so keen for us to enjoy life that he includes with his autobiography an invitation, a cheery, hopefully infectious invitation to live. In the words of the late Leslie Crowther from the British television programme *The Price is Right*, Solomon invites us to 'Come on down' – to go, to get up and live.

There is a call by Solomon for us to become rainbow people, those who live under the promise.

Now, to save confusion, what we need to be aware of is that such a disposition is not 'Life is so bad you may as well make the most of it,' a sort of fatalism. It is not 'Eat, drink and be merry, because tomorrow you might die.' Solomon has already dealt with this earlier. No, this is the perspective of the person of faith. This is why people become Christians.

This is the attitude of the one who lives under heaven. Here the attitude is not 'Eat, drink and be merry, for what else have you got?' or 'Live while you have the chance,' but rather, in the context of all the realities of life, 'Eat, drink and be merry, because …'

How do we live well?
Well, to be specific, Solomon says:

Firstly, enjoy socialising. Recently, we had some people back for lunch. We had an absolutely fantastic time. Like ourselves, these people have been in church ministry, so we had an awful lot that we could identify with. The wife comes from the same city as myself. We found out that she was co-leader of a Christian group in a school that our best man and one of my best friends led. Our children got on really well together. The food was great and the chat was excellent. Everything was good. I don't know about you, but I love those occasions – eating, laughing and chatting. Solomon says that's what you should be doing – that's life.

You know, the early church was known for such occasions. To those of us who go to church, communion has become a rather short, liturgical affair, but for the early church it was one of their biggest social get-togethers. The early church was known for its agape-love-meals and fellowship. Solomon says do likewise.

My wife's home church is famous for this type of thing. In fact, it needs no excuse to throw a party. Solomon says we should follow suit.

Secondly, enjoy your walk with God. One of the things that the first churches were characterised by was a holy passion. From one's reading of the New Testament it seems that, although not perfect, the early church was made up of those who were glad to be Christians; that it was a church where people were pleased to be attempting to be holy; where to be a fanatic for Christ was something to be desired and not scorned. Michael Green says that the early church was a hot place, where people were set on fire for Christ. Such a passion at Antioch got them the nickname 'Christ's ones', or Christians. The Christian faith was anything other than drudgery, boring, or something that you kept for yourself.

Solomon says that it should be so for us. His exhortation in this short section on how to have a good life is that, in regard to the spiritual, we should be those who enjoy their walk with God. He says 'Wear white clothes', which roughly means dress yourself in holiness, joyfully embrace such a quality in your life. It's a positive quality, not a negative one. And 'Anoint your head with oil', which means enter into and experience the presence of God. Don't be someone who knows that there is a God but feels that he is a million miles away. Experience right now God and the love that he has for you.

Thirdly, enjoy your life with your marriage partner. In the West we live in a society where marriage is becoming more and more out of fashion, where one in three of those who marry today can expect to find themselves divorced, where a substantial number of those who are married live with dead marriages. Although they are not divorced, they might as well be. They have lost the sparkle. They are in a state where, as I have already noted, many settle for a bit on the side instead of the best.

Solomon's advice to us is 'Don't settle for second best.' Enjoy your life with your husband or wife.

Many of us who are married will know that our loved one can be a mystery. From all the conversations I've had with married people I would question how many of us really understand our other half. He or she is a mystery unto him or herself, but what an adventure! Better than anything that Harrison Ford has ever starred in. And it is ours first-hand, a life with our partner. Just think about it: the same man or woman, twenty-four hours a day; seven days a week, fifty-two weeks of the year for potentially forty, fifty, sixty years.

If the sparkle has gone, then could I encourage you to talk with someone. If it has, or even if it hasn't, why not in the next month do one thing for your partner that you know he or she will love? To paraphrase the Apostle Paul, give yourself to the one you love. The outcome has the potential of being incredible.

Fourthly, enjoy your work, whether it be what you do in the office or at church, whether it is what you get paid for or do voluntarily. Enjoy it. Don't look for how you can skive off it and don't look for the easiest options. Give yourself to it and revel in it. In the words of business and management guru Tom Peters, 'live life out loud' in the workplace.

Why? Because one day, says Solomon, it will no longer be there for you.

> *in the grave, where you are going, there is neither working nor planning nor knowledge nor wisdom.*

Another way of interpreting the phrase 'white linen' is 'have your feasting gear on at all times'. Be truly alive. Solomon says, remember when you had a party outfit that you used to get out every now and then when you were going to have a really good time? Well, get it out now and party. Go on – become a party animal. When it comes to life, be OTT. Hug that tree. Seize the day – whether the ordinary or the special. Be as alive as you are on the morning of a major operation. For those of you who have ever had a major operation, or had to face the reality of possibly dying, Solomon says 'live' – see those flowers, feel the wind, see the sky.

To sum up, within the realities of life, what he says is don't live as if you have one foot in the grave.

The reason we should have such a disposition?

Some time ago, the then British Prime Minister John Major was asked how he thought the Conservatives would get on in the forthcoming General Election. He replied that they would win it.

'But why?' asked the interviewer. 'Why do you think they will win?' What were the reasons for his confidence? The polls showed that his party was a long way behind Labour, the mood of the nation was for change, the party had in recent days had to endure scandal after scandal. Why did he believe that the Conservatives would win? Where was such confidence coming from?

It's a good question. When the realities of life point to things being anything other than just short of bleak, what is the basis for confidence, for a disposition of joy? In his writings Solomon tells us what it is for the Christian. Think about these words: they will change your life.

The truth of life is that there is beauty and ugliness, more ugliness than beauty. The reason why we should rejoice is that we are 'in God's hands'.

Because the Lord is my shepherd, because I am under the care and supervision of Almighty God, because he is in control of my life, I can rejoice. He is one who is working in and through life's events for my good. He is one who, having begun a good work in me, will carry it on to completion. His are the hands that gave his son to die for me.

It might not seem it, sometimes impossible to believe it, but he is all these things for those who have ears to hear. To return to an earlier thought on how such is the uncertainty of life that we cannot be sure of whether we will be accepted or rejected by people, being in God's hands means that whatever others' response, we do not question God's commitment to us. We all need a three-dimensional view of life.

Are you in a singing mood? There was a story in the papers some time ago about how Pavarotti had lost his voice. I sometimes think that this is true of most people! There is a song, an old song, that tells us why we can have the disposition that Solomon encourages us to have in the context of the realities of life:

> *He's got the whole world in his hands.*

No, it does not answer all the questions of life, the mysteries, but it gives us confidence to know that there is reason and a purpose behind it even if this side of glory we don't know what it is. You know our quest for identity and meaning and explanation must end where Solomon's did, in the hands of God.

Whose hands are you in today? Do you know? A Christian is someone whose life is in God's hands.

When you know you are in the hands of God you can have a different view of suffering. In God's hands suffering becomes: educational – talk to Job, who learned a lot about his life and his friends as he went through a tough time; doxological – in being healed by God the blind man discovered the joy of worship; revelatory – Hosea discovered what God was like as he suffered through marital difficulties; sacrificial – Paul discovered the privileged place of serving others in his suffering; refining – talk to every Christian who has suffered. Suffering is, from God's perspective, an eternally long-term investment in you.

And how are we to view the uncertainties of life? For the Christian the word 'chance' in Solomon's autobiography should more accurately be interpreted 'events'. The words 'events' and 'time' carry with them the idea of control from external hands. You can guess whose hands they are.

In placing ourselves in God's hands, we have a foundation that will enable us to stand all the storms of life.

Conclusion

To return to the mirror: when I look in the mirror I see a man, a father, a husband, a son, a brother, a grandson, a dog owner, a Christian minister, me.

What I also see is 'God'. In particular, 'God in my life', strange as it might be to read or write. When I look in the mirror, as well as seeing all the other things that I have identified, I also see that God is in my life.

Sure, there needs to be more of him in our lives than there is, but nevertheless thank God for all that there is.

Can you see God in your life?

I can see God in the realities of life. In the difficult moments of death, whether pending or past, I can see him. In uncertainty I can see him. In the evil and insanity that resides within our world I can see him. In the midst of the good things that happen I can see him. Can you?

I can see God in how I live in the midst of these realities. He is the one who gives the greatest parties. He is the one who brings us into a relationship with himself and causes us to know fullness. He is the one who helps us enjoy our married life. He is the one who brings meaning to work. He is the one who dresses us with the greatest of all party outfits.

Tell me, does he do these things for you? Can you see him there?

Solomon told us that the basis for our response to the realities of life is that we are in God's hands. Jesus puts us there. Our walk with Jesus keeps us there.

When you look in the mirror, what is it that you see?

Chapter 10

God on ... the portrait of a fool

What does a fool look like?

Would you say a fool is like the model train fan who on the night of his wedding refuses to make love to his wife, preferring instead to try out a new track layout for his train set?

Would you say a fool is like the man who in the middle of a mid-life crisis leaves his wife for a school sweetheart, consequently losing the respect and company of his children and the woman who has been by his side for the last few decades?

Would you say a fool is like a footballer who on the eve of a major competition decided to row a boat from his homeland to that of the host nation?

In reading Solomon's autobiography it is obvious that he is concerned about the actions of the fool. Perhaps the reason for this is that he understands the consequences for people of acting like one. No one wants to see people ruin their or others' lives. As he says:

> As dead flies give perfume a bad smell,
> so a little folly outweighs wisdom and honour.

What I aim to do in this chapter is look at what Solomon has to say about fools, how he paints his portrait of a fool.

But before we do that, let me within my introduction make two comments about Solomon's portrait.

Firstly, it should be noted that there is no politically correct speaking here. Solomon is giving us some straight talk.

Secondly, Solomon's definition of a fool as someone whose heart inclines to the left instead of to the right is not a political statement. Rather, it is a statement based on how in Solomon's day the left stood for foolish, silly, wrong behaviour, and the right the complete opposite.

The disposition of the fool

A little while ago, the English football team Arsenal lost the European Cup Winners' Cup final in the last few minutes of the game because of a freak kick from forty yards out that caught the goalie off guard. He was out of position.

The fool, says Solomon, is someone who is out of position in life and so is unable to deal with the freak situations that he or she finds him or herself in; someone, says Solomon, who plays more like a centre forward than a goalie.

The particular situation that Solomon has in mind here is that of the office or factory floor, into which comes the boss, a boss who is not perfect. The particular faults of this boss are unjust anger and improper management.

> *If a ruler's anger rises against you ...*

> *Fools are put in many high positions ...*

Now, says Solomon, what should be your response in such a situation? What is the response of the fool?

Firstly, the fool takes the huff. This is the school playground attitude of 'You're not going to play with my ball.'

What Solomon is saying is, don't take this attitude. Don't resign, don't cut off your nose to spite your face. Don't respond to the boss in the same childlike manner that he of she is displaying to you. Realise that it is your boss who is at fault and not you.

Secondly, don't be impatient. Don't take the advice of a recent daily newspaper article and tell your boss the truth about him or herself. There is a Chinese proverb that says, 'If you are patient in one moment of anger, you will escape a hundred years of sorrow.'

Rather, says Solomon, in such a situation what you should do is take the disposition of the wise person. You should aim to bring calm into the situation. Calm can here be defined as healing. Try and pour oil on troubled waters. Do a Jesus to the wind and waves. Be like a kettle: 'though up to its neck in hot water, it continues to sing'.

I read a story recently about two men who got jobs in the complaints department of a well-known fashion store. As you can imagine, it was a tough job, and very quickly all the complaining, anger and threatening behaviour that the men were on the receiving end of discouraged them. It was so bad that their lives at home began to suffer.

One night after work they went to the pub to discuss what they could do. They felt that they had tried everything, but failed. They had fought back – but that only made matters worse. They had tried cold indifference – no change. They had tried patience – that failed too. What could they do? Should they resign?

As they stared around the room, groping for a way forward, their eyes fell upon a small plaque behind the bar, which read: 'Be kind, everyone you meet is fighting a tough battle.' And so they tried kindness. They took the lead and became courteous, they smiled and they helped.

They observed a few weeks later how a different class of customer now seemed to be coming to the store.

The mind of the fool

Those of you who play chess will know that in the game there is an opening called 'fool's mate'. Everyone who takes up the game gets caught with this opening. It's checkmate in four moves.

The fool is someone who never prepares in life for fool's mate, who is unprepared for life and the living of it; someone who doesn't think ahead and therefore always falls for the most obvious moves.

Solomon paints five scenes for us that would have had different outcomes if the person had thought ahead. In telling us of them, he informs us how the people all suffered because of presumption or assuming too much or not taking proper precautions or not thinking ahead.

Solomon says to us, living presents problems, so prepare. He tells us that in all probability one day our house will be broken into. So don't be a fool, take out the necessary insurance.

Secondly, says Solomon, work presents problems, so prepare. At a recent training day my wife's employers addressed the various difficult situations that their staff might find themselves in and how they should respond. Solomon says that the fool never concerns himself with such thoughts.

Thirdly, says Solomon, eternity presents us with problems, so don't be like the fool – prepare yourself. Since there is an eternal element to life, with a judgement that will determine your eternal destination, prepare for it, ready yourself for it.

The key word in this section is 'success'. Again and again, what Solomon is saying is, take the precautions necessary. Don't be unprepared.

The mouth of the fool

There was an interesting article in the Christian press recently about the number of fires in churches in London. Apparently during one spate one a week had to be dealt with. The fire brigade was so concerned about the statistics that it organised day conferences for churches on fire safety. It's all supposedly to do with electrical appliances.

But the Bible tells us about another way of starting a fire in the church or in one's personal life. It is done, says the book of James, through the speaking of unguarded words.

What Solomon tells us is that such words, coming from an unguarded tongue, are in fact the characteristics of a fool.

Solomon has a lot to say about the tongue and its taming. Proverbs, his other best-seller, is packed with sayings. Here he restricts himself to two.

Firstly, he tells us of the consequences for the fool of such unguarded words: he or she will be swallowed up by them and will end up on top of his or her own bonfire.

> *Words from a wise man's mouth are gracious,*
> *but a fool is consumed by his own lips.*

Secondly, we are told about the characteristics of unguarded words. They are unreasonable words. They just don't make sense. They are not logical. As Shakespeare writes in *Macbeth*, 'it is a tale told by an idiot, full of sound and fury, signifying nothing'. They are uncontrolled words. The fool can't stop saying things that he or she knows are wrong. They are boastful words. They speak much about the future, about that which no one understands.

The fool is one who not only doesn't guard his or her heart to prevent foolish words entering, but also someone who doesn't guard his or her heart to stop foolish ones getting out.

The actions and attitudes of the fool

Within the Bible there are many actions and attitudes recorded that the writers declare as those of the fool. There are those of the builder who builds his house on the sand, that of the farmer at retirement who puts his confidence and trust in what he has amassed as opposed to his eternal riches, that of the atheist with his conviction that there is no God.

In the final few verses of Ecclesiastes 10 we are given several more examples. Interestingly, they are all to do with middle managers – people who have others over them but also under them. What we are told is that foolish managers are those who are indulgent:

> *Woe to you, O land whose king was a servant*
> *and whose princes feast in the morning.*

These are managers who exploit the situation that they are in. In this situation the leader is portrayed as inexperienced, here called a servant or baby. Unaware of his or her duty, such a manager exploits the situation for his or her own gain.

In addition to being indulgent, Solomon tells us that foolish managers are also incompetent. They are those who do not or can not do what their job requires. Hence that which they are looking after begins to suffer.

As well as being indulgent and incompetent, Solomon tells us that foolish managers are also indifferent. They are those who live for everything other than what they are doing.

Finally, in addition to all of the aforementioned characteristics, Solomon tells us that foolish managers are also indiscreet. It is from what Solomon says that we get the well-known proverb 'a little bird told me so'. It is a fool who talks about his or her leaders, for those leaders are sure to find out what has been said.

Conclusion

Within the workplace no one wants to be considered somebody's fool. All want to make sure that they are in fact nobody's fool; that they know what is going on; that nobody is going to pull the wool over their eyes; that they are more than adequate for the job that they hold and are responsible for.

Solomon has informed us how to ensure that this is true for us; in how at work and in life, how in regard to those for whom we work and in regard to God, we must ensure that we are not fools.

Chapter 11

God on ... what life is all about

If someone were to ask you the question 'What do you believe life is all about?', what would you say?

You know, some people would say that life is all about doing noble acts that will leave their mark on the world. Many people want to leave a lasting impression on this world, a testimony that speaks of their contribution.

Some people would say that life is all about getting enough money to have a contented life and a comfortable retirement, appreciating that money makes the world go round, that money is the means to life. Some people believe that life is all about making their 'piggy bank' bigger and bigger.

Others would say that life is all about being able to stay the distance. Perhaps having lost a loved one, or perhaps having recently recovered from a severe medical condition, some believe that life is all about simply living as long as you can.

Those who accept the principle that life is all about engaging in the evolutionary process would say that life is all about bettering themselves, becoming the best that they can possibly be. We live in a world where everywhere people are being encouraged to better their looks, their dress sense, their education, their social skills, their jobs, their lovemaking.

If you are a parent you might say that life is all about making it possible for your kids to have the best possible start in life. When a friend of mine celebrated his twenty-first birthday, he inherited a substantial amount of money. Sensing the advantageous place that he was in he started his own business. All of us who have children would like to do that for them, to be able to give them a great head start in life. Some people believe that this is what life is all about.

If someone were to come up to you and ask you the question 'What is your life all about?', what would you say?

In the penultimate chapter of his autobiography, Solomon gives us his answer to this question. As I noted earlier, Ecclesiastes is Solomon's personal record of his quest to discover the answer to this very question, as well as the preliminary question of 'Is life worth living?'

Before I look at what Solomon says life is all about, I want firstly to mention two points about this chapter.

Firstly, what medium does Solomon adopt to communicate the answer to his question? We read that Solomon goes for seven proverbs that together illustrate his six-point principle for life.

Secondly, I will very briefly sum up what he has to say. His advice is, be bold, live by adventure. I am told that in Canada there is a sign at the start of a road that reads 'Choose your rut carefully. You are going to be in it for the next 200 miles.' For many people, that sign has proved to be a truth for their lives – they have been stuck in a rut for many a year. What Solomon does here is to show us how we can break out of that rut. How we can, to use the paraphrase in the J.B. Phillips Bible, 'let not the world squeeze us into its mould'.

Life is all about giving yourself away

One of my favourite stories in the Bible, a story that appears in all of the gospels, is the feeding of the 5000. Jesus has been teaching a large group of people about the way to live life. So captivated has been his audience and so keen has Jesus been to talk that the teaching session has gone on for a long time, well past meal time.

The disciples, aware that they are in a remote place, encourage Jesus to send the people home. But Jesus has other ideas. He tells the disciples to get all the people to sit down and then to feed them. But they can't, this is a remote place, there is not enough food to go around, they don't even have the money to buy food if there were a place that could serve them. Everything seems hopeless.

If you know the story, you will be aware that the day is saved by a young boy who gives his lunch of five loaves and two fish to Jesus. Jesus miraculously uses the boy's food to feed this large group.

That boy gave all that he had to Jesus. He gave his lunch away for the good of others despite the fact that it was so little compared with the need that existed, despite the fact that he would go without.

That boy had a choice: he could keep his food for himself, ensuring that he was OK, or he could give it up for others to benefit from, with no guarantee that he himself would benefit. Thankfully, for those there that day, he gave it to Jesus, who used it for the good of everyone.

Solomon says that the boy's choice of action is the decision that all of us should make in regard to our lives. We should all decide to give things away for others. That's what he is getting at in his proverb:

Cast your bread upon the waters ...

This was a Jewish, possibly Arab, proverb which expressed the view that it was better to give something away as opposed to hoarding it. What Solomon is encouraging here is that we get involved in 'letting go' of that which we have gripped on to and which grips us.

Have you ever asked yourself the question, 'What is a Christian?' A Christian, according to Jesus, is someone who has carried through this principle to God and then sought to live it out to others.

This is the definition Jesus gave when he was talking to the disciples. In Matthew 16, just after Peter's confession at Caesarea Philippi that Jesus was indeed the promised one from God, Jesus informed the disciples that if anyone would be his follower that they must be willing to:

> *deny himself and take up his cross and follow me.*

What this roughly means is that if you want to be one of Jesus' followers then you must be willing to give yourselves to God.

According to Solomon, this 'losing of your life' is the key to finding life. It is something that was said by a second-century theologian to be the chief end of humankind.

For those of us who consider such a request a bit harsh, we are encouraged in the New Testament to observe how this was the example that Christ himself has set us. Paul lists for us seven ways in which Jesus gave himself away to others. He says that Jesus:

> *did not consider equality with God*
> *something to be grasped,*
> *but made himself nothing,*
> *taking the very nature of a servant,*
> *being made in human likeness.*

> *And being found in appearance as a man,*
> *he humbled himself*
> *and became obedient to death*
> *— even death on a cross!*

What Solomon is encouraging us to do is to follow Jesus' example.

The Bible tells us that we are not talking of foolish actions. Jim Elliot, a famous missionary, once said:

> *He is no fool who gives what he cannot keep to gain that*
> *which he cannot lose.*

Jesus Christ said:

> *whoever wants to save his life will lose it, but whoever loses*
> *his life for me and for the gospel will save it.*

If anything, this is the best investment that one can make with one's life. It is the one that offers the best returns, not only in this life but also in the life to come.

Now, being the wise man that he is, Solomon is aware that it is important not to leave people without a knowledge of how to give of themselves. So, in the context of encouraging us to give ourselves away, he gives us an illustration of one of the ways that we could do this. It is an illustration that is sure to raise immediate interest.

The inference in the proverb of 11:1 is that it is in alms giving, in the giving of one's money away to help those in need, that we can give ourselves away to others.

In the Bible, a person's use of money says a lot about that person. For one thing, it tells us where that person's heart is. Solomon says that using your money in other people's lives is a good place to begin giving yourself away.

Solomon says, in regard to our hard-earned money, that life is all about giving it away as opposed to depositing it in our own personal bank account. Don't be a bigger barn builder – be a Saint Nicholas.

The first part of the answer to what is life all about is that it is about giving yourself away to others, in particular investing your money wisely in others.

Life is all about giving ourselves away, wholeheartedly

Several years ago when I was the leader of a church in Scotland I entered a golf tournament. Although a complete novice at golf, I was encouraged by several of my friends to enter the competition. They told me that several other ministers were playing in the tournament, that there was a handicap system that ensured that the worst players got the biggest head start and that they wanted me to take part in the day.

Aware of my own inadequacies on the golf course, in preparation for the event I asked one of my friends to take me out and give me some coaching.

Harry's first bit of advice was to withdraw from playing in the tournament. When he realised that people expected me to be there, his second bit of advice was that when I swung the club, particularly as I teed off, he felt that I should slow down a bit, exercising a bit more control and less power. Whereas I wanted to give it everything I had, Harry saw that we got better results when I was less powerful and more controlled – I actually made contact with the ball.

Solomon says that when it comes to discovering what life is all about Harry's advice is the wrong advice. It might be OK for the golf course, but not for living.

Solomon says that life is all about giving yourself away wholeheartedly. He says:

> *Give portions to seven, yes to eight ...*

This means give all that you have got *ad infinitum*. It is a proverb that encourages total, over-the-top giving.

In the early church believers, generally at their baptism, confessed that 'Jesus is Lord'. In acknowledging Jesus as Lord of their lives they were accrediting him with the highest status given in those days, akin to supreme emperor. What they were also doing was saying that from this day forth they were going to live their lives for Jesus. From now on he would be the controller of their lives. It would be his standards, his demands, him that they would seek to please. What Solomon is saying is that life is all about the living of it as if Jesus were Lord of everything.

An interesting comment that someone once made was that if he wasn't Lord of all, then he wasn't Lord at all.

To quote Admiral James T. Kirk in *Star Trek*, with regard to life it is 'Full ahead, Mr Sulu.' It is about no longer hanging a 'Do not disturb' sign over your life.

To pick up on Solomon's earlier application on how this works out with regard to our money, what he is saying is that we are to be like the woman Jesus spoke about. Although she only gave two small coins, she gave all out of her poverty, as opposed to the rich man who, although he gave more, gave little out of his plenty.

When I was a teenager, every Boxing Day fifteen lads from the churches of the town that I belonged to would take on fifteen lads from the neighbouring town in a game of rugby. So fierce was the game that the next day it was not uncommon for most of the lads from both towns to be unable to walk. You see, in the game, both teams gave everything. No one held anything back. There was no place for players to act as spectators, no place for people not to give their all. We all wanted to win and we all knew that it demanded everything from us if we were going to succeed.

Solomon says that life is all about giving yourself away wholeheartedly, to God first and then to your neighbour.

Life is all about giving yourself away, wholeheartedly, irrespective of our present situation and of the future risks involved

As I've said, one of the things that drives my wife up the wall is that I usually promise to do things later. The problem is, of course, is that later never comes. When she asks me to cut the grass – later. When she asks me to fix the broken tables – later, normally after they have collapsed with something on them making a mess on the carpet.

When it comes to giving ourselves away wholeheartedly to God and to each other, Solomon knows that 'later' is a phrase that many of us often use. Although in principle we see the wisdom of an action and have the initial desire to carry it out, for a variety of reasons we put it off. 'I'll

do it when I'm older ... when things change ... when I've
got more time ... when we've paid off this overdraft ...
when the kids have grown up ... when work becomes
quieter.'

Aware of our tendency to procrastinate – to put off
till tomorrow what should be done today – Solomon
encourages us to see that procrastination is, in fact, one of
the great thieves in our spiritual lives.

What the particular excuse in Solomon's mind that
he is seeking to defeat is we are not told. From the
illustrations used we might suggest that it is those of
we-don't-know-what-the-future-holds or circumstances-
at-the-moment-don't-really-lend-themselves-to-such-a-
lifestyle excuses.

Whatever, what he says is, if the truth be told, the ideal
situation never comes. Therefore don't be deterred:

> *Whoever watches the wind will not plant;*
> *whoever looks at the clouds will not reap.*

Half of the word 'life' is the word 'if'. Solomon says don't
make judgements on the 'if'. What he is saying is that the
God who gave us necks expects us to stick them out once
in a while.

It is doubtful that Moses would ever have left Egypt if
he had looked only at the circumstances. Pharaoh wasn't
keen on the idea. There were lots of people to lead. Who
knew whether they would work together? Would he have
ever attempted to walk through the water? Would he have
ever been prepared to wander in the desert for forty years?
But he did it despite the circumstances. Solomon urges us
to take his example.

Jesus told the story of a landowner who was going away
for a long holiday. Before he left, this man gave three of

his stewards different sums of money to invest for him while he was away. To one he gave five talents (a talent was a weight of currency), to another two talents and to another one talent.

When he returned from his travels he gathered the stewards together and asked them to report on their activities. The one who had been given five talents told how he had gathered five more, the one who had been given two how he had earned two more. The one who had been given one simply returned that sum.

The landowner asked this last employee what he had done with the money to have made no appreciation on it. The man's reply was that he had buried it. He was frightened of the owner and was scared of losing the money. That man received the landowner's condemnation, the other two his recommendation.

Jesus told this story to encourage all of us to make best use of what we have been given, not to bury it, not to be half-hearted in our use of it. We too can sometimes be intimidated by circumstances. Solomon advises us not to let them prevent us from giving ourselves whole-heartedly.

Solomon tells us to give all, whole-heartedly, irrespective of the outward circumstances, not recklessly, but having thought about our situation, realising that some things one can never be sure of.

Life is all about giving yourself away, whole-heartedly, irrespective of the present situation or of the future risks involved, as an act of faith

In the biblical book of Acts, we read of a disciple who went AWOL – absent without leave. Mark, who had accompanied the first two Christians sent out by the church on a missionary journey, decided to turn back.

Mark is like many spiritually orientated people today who have started their journey well but who because of circumstances, because of the 'wind and the waves', pull out.

To those of us who have thought or acted like Mark, Solomon gives us his reasons as to why we should stay with our spiritual journey, the very basis on which such giving away of ourselves should be done; why we should not become another Mark.

Solomon says we should stay with it because we can trust God. Yes, there is so much that we do not know – the path of the wind, the formation of a baby, the work of God. However, what we do know is that because we do not know we should not withhold our hand.

Why? Because we know that unless we sow we will not reap and because God commands us to sow.

So, if God has given us opportunity to do it, that is what we should do. We cannot have confidence in what the result will be – it could be either positive or negative. Yet we must do it because we have been told to.

Anyway, when has it ever been about having a positive or negative outcome? If one looks at the heroes of faith listed in Hebrews 11, they were heroes if they came in the first part of the list (those who saw what they hoped for realised) or the second half of the list (those who died with their vision of what could and would be unfulfilled).

We do it all, says Solomon, in the belief that God is in it and will lead us through it. If he has given us opportunity to give, to sow, then we must.

Life is all about giving yourself away, wholeheartedly, irrespective of the present situation or of the future risks involved, as an act of faith, with a sense of urgency

One of the books written by the American sociologist Tony Campolo is entitled *Carpe Diem*:[8] 'seize the day' is the translation of this Latin phrase.

The book is an encouragement by Campolo to live in the now of life. Perhaps sensing that many people are apathetic about living, Campolo exhorts us to seize the day in our marriages, with our children, in our work and in what we have determined to make our life mission statement – to seize the day in everything. There is in Campolo's book a sense of urgency to embrace the now.

This is Solomon's advice to us. We should seize the day, have a sense of urgency about our living, grasp what is to be grasped now and not later. Solomon says live as one:

who does not know what disaster will come upon the land.

We are to live as though one day there will be a loss of opportunity. Jesus says the Kingdom of God is near. Solomon says grab it. The Apostle Paul says today is the day of salvation. Solomon says embrace it.

Solomon tells us to be like the blind man who heard that Jesus was going by and decided to shout and shout as if his life depended on it. His friends exhorted him not to draw attention to himself, not to distract the Master, but he was having none of it. He knew that if life was to be lived,

---

[8] Tony Campolo, *Carpe Diem* (Word, 1994).

if he was to receive his sight, then he needed Jesus. And Jesus was walking by now. Now was the time to shout. Hear the urgency in his voice.

He tells us to be like Peter and John, who had a race to see who could get to the tomb first. Was it true that Jesus was alive? If he was, then he might be there. There was no time to sit around; it was time to run with all their might to see if they could see him.

Or we should be like Peter who, several days after the death and resurrection of Jesus, whilst out fishing, saw Jesus on the shore and before anyone could stop him was in the water and swimming to his best friend, desperate to get there before he disappeared again?

When in Dublin recently, I came across a word that I had never heard before: 'mañana', which in Spanish means 'tomorrow'. This word was being used in Dublin in the context of 'later ... not now ... in a little while ... tomorrow'. What Solomon and what Campolo say is that if life is to be truly lived then there is no place in our lives for 'mañana'. We should live with a sense of urgency.

Life is all about giving yourself away, wholeheartedly, irrespective of our present situation and of the future risks involved, as an act of faith, with a sense of urgency, with the assurance of his promise

What is the promise? Solomon tells us it is that:

> *after many days you will find it again.*

Which roughly means what you sow you will reap.

In addition to that, if one understands Jesus right, there will also be a multiplication factor. As Jesus said:

unless a grain of wheat falls to the ground and dies, it remains only a single seed. But if it dies, it produces many seeds.

The truth of this could be heard if we were to talk to the mother of the boy who gave his food to Jesus. She sent him out in the morning with five loaves and two small fish. Who knows how much of the twelve baskets that were left over, after Jesus had used that food to feed the 5000 men, women and children, he brought home with him. It would be interesting to talk to their neighbours about all the bread they were given that week and the fish smell next door and in the street.

We see this multiplication factor in the life of an Old Testament character called Caleb. For fifty years Caleb had honoured God in the way that he had lived and believed. His reward at the end of them was an inheritance of land and an eternal testimony. He had sown in faith; he had reaped materially and spiritually.

Obviously, there is no guarantee when it will come back to you, but it will. We should not get in a tizzy if we have to wait for the other side – all the better. One day we will all stand before Jesus, face to face with the crucified one, an awesome day. It will be absolutely fabulous to hear him say 'Well done' and to see him smile and give you a crown, to look at his face and see the eyes of one who is pleased with you.

Solomon says God's promise is there:

after many days you will find it again.

What an exhilarating basis to give your life.

Conclusion

One day, in many senses an ordinary day in the life of Jesus, whilst teaching his followers about the kingdom, Jesus said that he had come so that we:

> *might have life, and that ... abundantly.* (KJB)

I don't know about you, but as far as I am concerned, I want that sort of life. I want life abundantly. I want to know what it means to be truly alive.

Solomon tells us that such a life is to be found in giving yourself away, wholeheartedly, irrespective of your present situation and of the future risks involved, as an act of faith, with a sense of urgency, with the assurance of his promise. You know our world needs people who will live that way. You and I need to live that way.

May God, the giver of life, give us the ability to make the first steps in this greatest of adventures.

Chapter 12

God on … a mystery solved

Who did it and why? That was the question, it seemed, on everyone's mind as they gathered in the dining car of the Orient Express. It had been seventy-two hours since the body of Mr Ratchett had been found in his locked cabin, stabbed twelve times.

They had all, when called, given an account of their whereabouts that night and offered, in most cases, their opinions as to why the crime had been committed and by whom. Unfortunately, the statements had not pointed to any particular person. It seemed that everyone had an alibi.

The owner of the train and the doctor who had pro-nounced the victim dead held no hope of the crime being solved. Now it was up to Hercule Poirot, the world-renowned Belgian detective, to solve what to everyone else seemed insoluble.

As in most Agatha Christie novels, when Poirot explained who had done it and why, the conclusion was surprising and yet obvious.

We come to the final comments in Solomon's journal. As I expressed in Chapter 1, his was a journal in which he started to record his personal investigation into the death of 'a meaningless life'. For the last eleven chapters we have sat with Solomon, this Old Testament detective, as he has investigated the crime, interviewed the witnesses and interrogated the suspects. We have been with him as he has looked at the corpse, the dead body of 'a meaningless life'. We have gone with him to the police station to look at the various suspects in the line-up. Who killed 'a meaningless life'? Was it materialism, a liberated sexuality, pleasure, wisdom or folly? We have, with him, seen how each of these has proved to be innocent.

> *Then I applied myself to the understanding of wisdom, and also of madness and folly, but I learned that this, too, is a chasing after the wind.*

We come now to the conclusion of the matter, how he solved the mysterious death of 'a meaningless life' or, to put it in the positive, how exactly do we get a life worth living? As was Hercule Poirot's, Solomon's conclusion is surprising and yet obvious.

What I want to do is look with you at how the crime was committed. We are going to attempt to identify the murderer.

Before we look at what Solomon gives us as his surprising and yet obvious conclusion, I want to identify within my introduction several facts about the case.

Firstly, in regard to the detective who will volunteer the conclusion, the passage tells us that he was more than qualified to investigate the crime. We are told that he was a man of wisdom and experience. This is not the first time that he has had to think such complicated cases through.

> *Not only was the Teacher wise, but also he imparted knowledge to the people. He pondered and searched out and set in order many proverbs.*

Secondly, that in regard to his method for gaining information, we would be right in saying that at times he has been provocative and ruthless. He was more than willing to goad his witnesses. He was determined to get at the truth and, it seems, to ensure that the truth got at us.

Thirdly, in regard to the evidence, we should know that he has studied and searched all things. There is not a piece of information that has not been discovered. Hence he can say:

Now all has been heard; here is the conclusion to the matter ...

Fourthly, in regard to his conclusion, it is transferable to all such cases. We live in an age where truth has become relative. People tell us that it might be true for you but not me. One person's drink is another person's poison. When it comes to solving the mysterious death of 'a meaningless life' the same answer is for everyone. There is no one for whom this is not relevant. No one. There is no possibility of a wrongful arrest. If you are wanting to have your 'meaningless life' murdered, then Solomon's suspect will be able to do it for you.

OK then, so what is Israel's Hercule Poirot's conclusion to the crime that will never be featured on the television or in the theatre, yet should be, for it is the greatest crime of all time? Who killed 'a meaningless life'?

Well, says Solomon, the crime was carried out by a five-strong team.

Focus on God

When it comes to killing 'a meaningless life', this is done when we give ourselves to and for something. In Solomon's words, that something is our Creator.

Remember your Creator ...

In Ecclesiastes 3 Solomon tells us that there is within each one of us a sense of eternity, a sense of the divine, the spiritual, it is something that God has put within us. Pascal called it a God-shaped hole. It is a hole that nothing in this world can fill. What Solomon is saying is that the hole is filled when we give ourselves to and for our Creator.

This action of giving oneself to God is summed up in Solomon's word *'Remember'*. In Hebrew, to remember means more than engaging in a mental act of recollection or occasional reflection or superficial remembrance, it means to give yourself to something. It means turning your attention to God and realising that you are in need of him and so you drop your pretence of self-sufficiency and determine to give yourself to and for him. It means to focus on him; to become passionately loyal to him; to act decisively for him. To give it a New Testament feel, it means to 'seek ye first the kingdom of God' (KJV). It is akin to Jesus' encouragement to build our house on the rock, to sell all to buy the field with the buried treasure in.

Interestingly, Solomon's exhortation is that we do such a giving of ourselves now. He is keen that we do not procrastinate, put off till tomorrow what we can do today. Our author realises that, for many, 'later' never comes.

Solomon is particularly concerned that those of us who are young do it now. His thinking seems to be that it is easier to determine to follow the ways of God in one's youth rather than when one is old.

in the days of your youth ...

He is keen that we do it before the winter of life sets in. I haven't got the space to go into it, but in Ecclesiastes 12

Solomon gives us some of the most glorious descriptions of old age ever written. If you have time, read it and see if you can work out the allusions. The key is in seeing a house as symbolism for the body.

In his explanation of the parable of the sower, Jesus tells us that there are many reasons why people delay or why they put off altogether making such a decision. Some don't give themselves to God because trouble or persecution comes their way; others don't go with it because of the worries of this life or the riches of this life or even because the pleasures of this life are too enticing for them.

Solomon, the realist, knew that life's pleasures could tempt his readers, then and now, to procrastinate. So in the midst of exhorting people to give themselves, he is also pragmatic enough to give them the reasons why they should.

Why should we give ourselves to God?

Firstly, because of the fragility of life and the certainty of death. One day we will all die. One day we will be no more, before that day we owe it to ourselves to truly live.

Secondly, because of the immortality of the soul. Those of you who saw the film *Field of Dreams* will know that the characters had to wrestle with the concept of there being a life after death. Solomon tells us that such a concept is true, that there is a life after death. In the light of this we should give ourselves to God and so have a life worth living forever.

Thirdly, because of the meaninglessness of life. Everything that society says makes for life doesn't. The problem is that most people spend their lives never realising the lie. You can have it all, but you will not be satisfied.

Fourthly, because of the surprise of death. A long time ago I conducted an evangelistic meeting for young people. Three days after my meeting one of the young people, while crossing the road on his way home from school, was knocked down and killed. So young, so much of life left, but it was snatched away. Such, says Solomon, could be the case for us. The particular illustration he paints in these verses is that of the heart attack victim. Suddenly it could all be over. Solomon warns us not to delay.

How do we have a life worth living? How do we kill 'a meaningless life'? What is the key to breaking out of the Colditz of boredom and futility and meaninglessness? Solomon tells us it is by giving ourselves to God. Have you done that? Are you still doing it?

Fear God

Every one of us was created by God to have a relationship with him. The way that we murder 'a meaningless life' is by developing a relationship with this God. In particular, we see the end of futility when we enter into a relationship with God wherein we fear him.

It is important to note that to fear God does not mean to have a relationship in which we are filled with terror. To fear God means, in essence, to have a right, true, good, free and fun relationship with God. It means to see him as he truly is and worship him as a result of it.

The pop singer Yazz told us that 'the only way is up'. As Solomon says, 'Focus on God.' What he also says is that when you focus ensure that you get a proper vision, for from such a vision will come a life worth living.

As those of you who have read the passage will know, Solomon does not tell us how our fear of God kills 'a meaningless life'. For that we have to go into the New Testament where we are told by one who knows, Jesus, that to know God is synonymous with having eternal life, a life that is qualitative and quantitative.

It seems to me that the greatest need for all of us is to come to fear God, to get that right relationship with him. I believe, and the Bible teaches us, that it is the most important thing about us, it is what transforms our lives.

It is time to see that God forgives you. You have done things in your life that have weighed you down with guilt. The Bible teaches that, through Jesus, God can forgive you your sins.

It is time to see that God loves you. You feel worthless; your life is filled with worry and anxiety. You believe that no one loves you. You know what you are like and, although you know that God so loved the world that he gave his Son, you just can't believe that that love is for you. You need to experience that love.

It is time to see that God is for you. As you walk through life he is at your side clapping and cheering you on.

It is time to see that God has a plan for you. When you come to believe in Jesus, you will see that God has something for you to do that will last for eternity.

Solomon tells us that the death of 'a meaningless life' is found in a right relationship with God. It is found in the fear of God. Someone once said that if you fear God you fear nothing else, but if you don't fear God you fear everything else.

Imagine a life without debilitating fear. Such a life worth living comes from the fear of God.

Follow the commandments of God

What are you like at taking other people's advice? Are you more than willing to take on board what people have to say to you? Do you find yourself thinking 'I know better' and so proceed on what you think is the best course?

A couple of months ago I came to the conclusion that it was right to have a charity newsletter printed. Our aim was that the brochure would be used to inform people of what we were doing, how we were thinking and what we hoped might be opening up. We intended to send it to about a hundred of our friends and family and then use it at the churches that I speak at.

Because of the importance of the brochure we decided to have it professionally printed. To say the least, we had a disastrous time. When we saw it our hearts sank. I felt sick. There were spelling mistakes, there were sentences missing and the colour was not what we agreed on. Although we had given the printer a perfect original he had not followed it.

What made matters worse was that all this need not have happened. You see, as we were putting our brochure together, one of our friends gave us some advice on how to deal with printers. He had worked with this strange breed of creature before and from his mistakes he knew what should and should not be done. Paul, thinking he knew better, decided not to heed his advice. The second time, when my friend spoke to me, I took notes.

Solomon says that when it comes to the death of 'a meaningless life' the secret is found in having a sponge-like attitude. It is being someone who is ready and willing to soak up advice. What he is talking about here is having a teachable spirit, being an individual who has an open mind and heart. The call here is for enrolment in further educational training. In particular and exclusively one has to listen to the advice of God.

Solomon says that you get a life worth living by following the Maker's instructions. Since we were created by God, as our Maker he knows best. The best thing we can do therefore is follow what he says.

keep his commandments ...

What Solomon is saying is learn to play 'Simple Simon' with God. He says it, so we should do it. If nothing else it will remove us from that stagnant pool that we find ourselves in.

In the newspaper sometime ago there was an article by Carol Thatcher. She was writing to the new inhabitants of 10 Downing Street, the home of the British Prime Minister. In the article she gave her advice on how best to live in the house. What Solomon says is that God has written such advice for us on life. We should heed it.

Now, in following the Maker's instructions, it is important that we do not fall into two of the traps that will prevent us from fully benefiting from this lifestyle.

Firstly, that of embracing such on an external level. One of the groups of people that Jesus spoke against when he was on earth was that which tried to follow God's laws externally but not internally, religious people who tried to do the actions but not develop the heart. Such people he viewed as hypocritical. What is more, they missed out on the good life.

Secondly, seeing such as a means of earning our salvation. What we are talking about here is not how you might win favour in God's eyes; rather, how you might enjoy the glorious gift of new life that he has given us. We develop such a lifestyle because we see it as the wise way to live. This is pragmatic living. It is the best way to live.

As to the parameters of God's guidelines, the New Testament teaches us they incorporate every issue of life. God's guide for living includes the family, our relationships, what we do at work and how our church is run. If you want to know how to best bring up your children – read the Bible. If you want to know how to conduct a good relationship – read the Bible. If you want to know what to look for in a partner – read the Bible. If you want to know how to rescue a relationship – read the Bible. If you want to know how to behave at work – read the Bible. If you want to know how to be a good boss, a good employee – read the Bible. If you want to know how to run a good church – read the Bible. If you want to be a better individual – read the Bible.

One of the memorable lines of comedy duo Morecambe and Wise is Eric's invitation to Ernie to 'walk this way'. Such is Solomon's invitation to us. How do we murder 'a meaningless life'? Ensure that we walk this way – God's way.

Face the Future

When I worked with an Episcopal church in Edinburgh we organised a youth camp called 'The Party'. The camp was excellent.

One of the things that made it so was our after-hours programme, in particular one of the items we did called 'Squirm with Smith'. The way it worked was that my friend

Adrian invited one of the camp audience up to the stage and there, having sat him or her down and begun to make him or her feel comfortable, turned the interview into an interrogation.

The way he did this was by showing on our video screen our filming of the unsuspecting person's house, which we had gained access to the week before. In front of all of his or her friends and usually family, we revealed the state of the rooms, what was in some of the drawers, any cuddly toys, any posters that could cause embarrassment. And occasionally we would discover a love letter that he or she had written or received (normally written and planted by us). Then, after the video had finished and the interviewee was just getting over the shock, Adrian would continue with the interview, this time asking embarrassing questions, sourced from parents and school friends, in the style of the television show *This is your Life*. As you can imagine, 'Squirm with Smith' was an apt name.

What Solomon says in Ecclesiastes 12 is that such an encounter will one day be ours. With my friend Adrian Smith – no. But with God. According to Solomon, every one of us is going to stand face to face with our Maker. Unfortunately, it is not going to be as much fun as 'Squirm with Smith':

> For God will bring every deed into judgement ...

When we planned our squirm sessions we tried our best to get all the information we could on our victim. It will be nothing to what God will have on us. Solomon says that our judgement will be on every deed:

> including every hidden thing, whether it is good or evil.

With regard to what this has to do with the death of 'a meaningless life', it is that as we live in the light of our eternal judgement we come to live a life worth living. We are one day going to stand face to face with God. Life is therefore more than three score years and ten and then nothing – rather, life ever after. What you do here has repercussions on the other side. A life worth living is a life worth living in the light of eternity.

Are you investing in eternity? At present there are no exchange rates that allow you to take the wealth that you acquire on this side to the other side.

One of the things that marked the early Christians was this concept of living in the light of eternity. We are told it was this hope that kept them going through the tough times. It conditioned every day that they lived. It gave an overwhelming urgency to life.

Tell me, does this mark your living, as it did theirs?

Conclusion

One day, many years after Solomon had died, there came to the Temple that he had built a man, a Jewish man, who in many senses looked like everyone else. This man had come to the Temple because he had a confession to make, a confession that was to cost him his life.

The man had come to confess to the crime that Solomon had investigated. He was the fifth man, the ringleader who had planned the death of 'a meaningless life'. In fact, it had been he who had plunged the dagger in.

It was he and he alone who was the murderer, the others were but accomplices. He had never been accused and arrested by Solomon because Solomon had never discovered his involvement. But now he felt was the right time to make his confession.

We read his confession in the Gospel of John 7:37:

On the last and greatest day of the Feast, Jesus stood and said in a loud voice, 'If anyone is thirsty, let him come to me and drink. Whoever believes in me, as the Scripture has said, streams of living water will flow from within him.'

I want to finish by asking you a very personal but specific question. Are you thirsty? In your own life, do you want to see 'a meaningless life' murdered? Do you want to have a life worth living?

Jesus says to all of us, if you are thirsty, then come to me and drink. Do you want to drink?

To all of us, Jesus says, 'I did it. I murdered a meaningless life. I did it and I'm glad I did it. It needed to be done. Do you want me to do it in your life?'

Appendix

The ancient manuscript of Ecclesiastes

New International Version

Ecclesiastes 1

Everything is meaningless

¹ The words of the Teacher, son of David, king of Jerusalem:

² 'Meaningless! Meaningless!'
says the Teacher.
'Utterly meaningless!
Everything is meaningless.'

³ What does man gain from all his labour
at which he toils under the sun?
⁴ Generations come and generations go,
but the earth remains for ever.
⁵ The sun rises and the sun sets,
and hurries back to where it rises.
⁶ The wind blows to the south
and turns to the north;
round and round it goes,
ever returning on its course.
⁷ All streams flow into the sea,
yet the sea is never full.
To the place the streams come from,
there they return again.
⁸ All things are wearisome,
more than one can say.

The eye never has enough of seeing,
nor the ear its fill of hearing.
⁹ What has been will be again,
what has been done will be done again;
there is nothing new under the sun.
¹⁰ Is there anything of which one can say,
'Look! This is something new'?
It was here already, long ago;
it was here before our time.
¹¹ There is no remembrance of men of old,
and even those who are yet to come
will not be remembered
by those who follow.

Wisdom is meaningless

¹² I, the Teacher, was king over Israel in Jerusalem. ¹³ I
devoted myself to study and to explore by wisdom all that
is done under heaven. What a heavy burden God has laid
on men! ¹⁴ I have seen all the things that are done under the
sun; all of them are meaningless, a chasing after the wind.

¹⁵ What is twisted cannot be straightened;
what is lacking cannot be counted.

¹⁶ I thought to myself, 'Look, I have grown and increased in
wisdom more than anyone who has ruled over Jerusalem
before me; I have experienced much of wisdom and
knowledge.' ¹⁷ Then I applied myself to the understanding
of wisdom, and also of madness and folly, but I learned that
this, too, is a chasing after the wind.

¹⁸ For with much wisdom comes much sorrow;
the more knowledge, the more grief.

Ecclesiastes 2

Pleasures are meaningless

¹ I thought in my heart, 'Come now, I will test you with
pleasure to find out what is good.' But that also proved to

be meaningless. [2] 'Laughter,' I said, 'is foolish. And what does pleasure accomplish?' [3] I tried cheering myself with wine, and embracing folly – my mind still guiding me with wisdom. I wanted to see what was worth while for men to do under heaven during the few days of their lives.

[4] I undertook great projects: I built houses for myself and planted vineyards. [5] I made gardens and parks and planted all kinds of fruit trees in them. [6] I made reservoirs to water groves of flourishing trees. [7] I bought male and female slaves and had other slaves who were born in my house. I also owned more herds and flocks than anyone in Jerusalem before me. [8] I amassed silver and gold for myself, and the treasure of kings and provinces. I acquired men and women singers, and a harem as well – the delights of the heart of man. [9] I became greater by far than anyone in Jerusalem before me. In all this my wisdom stayed with me.

[10] I denied myself nothing my eyes desired;
I refused my heart no pleasure.
My heart took delight in all my work,
and this was the reward for all my labour.
[11] Yet when I surveyed all that my hands had done
and what I had toiled to achieve,
everything was meaningless, a chasing after the wind;
nothing was gained under the sun.

Wisdom and folly are meaningless

[12] Then I turned my thoughts to consider wisdom,
and also madness and folly.
What more can the king's successor do
than what has already been done?
[13] I saw that wisdom is better than folly,
just as light is better than darkness.
[14] The wise man has eyes in his head,
while the fool walks in the darkness;
but I came to realise
that the same fate overtakes them both.

¹⁵ Then I thought in my heart,

> 'The fate of the fool will overtake me also.
> What then do I gain by being wise?'
> I said in my heart,
> 'This too is meaningless.'

¹⁶ For the wise man, like the fool, will not be long
remembered;
in days to come both will be forgotten.
Like the fool, the wise man too must die!

Toil is meaningless

¹⁷ So I hated life, because the work that is done under the sun
was grievous to me. All of it is meaningless, a chasing after
the wind. ¹⁸ I hated all the things I had toiled for under the
sun, because I must leave them to the one who comes after
me. ¹⁹ And who knows whether he will be a wise man or a
fool? Yet he will have control over all the work into which
I have poured my effort and skill under the sun. This too
is meaningless. ²⁰ So my heart began to despair over all
my toilsome labour under the sun. ²¹ For a man may do
his work with wisdom, knowledge and skill, and then he
must leave all he owns to someone who has not worked for
it. This too is meaningless and a great misfortune. ²² What
does a man get for all the toil and anxious striving with
which he labours under the sun? ²³ All his days his work is
pain and grief; even at night his mind does not rest. This
too is meaningless.

²⁴ A man can do nothing better than to eat and drink and find
satisfaction in his work. This too, I see, is from the hand of
God, ²⁵ for without him, who can eat or find enjoyment?
²⁶ To the man who pleases him, God gives wisdom,
knowledge and happiness, but to the sinner he gives the
task of gathering and storing up wealth to hand it over
to the one who pleases God. This too is meaningless, a
chasing after the wind.

Ecclesiastes 3

A time for everything

1 There is a time for everything,
and a season for every activity under heaven:

2 a time to be born and a time to die,
a time to plant and a time to uproot,
3 a time to kill and a time to heal,
a time to tear down and a time to build,
4 a time to weep and a time to laugh,
a time to mourn and a time to dance,
5 a time to scatter stones and a time to gather them,
a time to embrace and a time to refrain,
6 a time to search and a time to give up,
a time to keep and a time to throw away,
7 a time to tear and a time to mend,
a time to be silent and a time to speak,
8 a time to love and a time to hate,
a time for war and a time for peace.

9 What does the worker gain from his toil? 10 I have seen the burden God has laid on men. 11 He has made everything beautiful in its time. He has also set eternity in the hearts of men; yet they cannot fathom what God has done from beginning to end. 12 I know that there is nothing better for men than to be happy and do good while they live. 13 That everyone may eat and drink, and find satisfaction in all his toil – this is the gift of God. 14 I know that everything God does will endure forever; nothing can be added to it and nothing taken from it. God does it so that men will revere him.

15 Whatever is has already been,
and what will be has been before;
and God will call the past to account.

16 And I saw something else under the sun:

In the place of judgement – wickedness was there,
in the place of justice – wickedness was there.

¹⁷ I thought in my heart,

> 'God will bring to judgement
> both the righteous and the wicked,
> for there will be a time for every activity,
> a time for every deed.'

¹⁸ I also thought, 'As for men, God tests them so that they may see that they are like the animals. ¹⁹ Man's fate is like that of the animals; the same fate awaits them both: As one dies, so dies the other. All have the same breath; man has no advantage over the animal. Everything is meaningless. ²⁰ All go to the same place; all come from dust, and to dust all return. ²¹ Who knows if the spirit of man rises upward and if the spirit of the animal goes down into the earth?'

²² So I saw that there is nothing better for a man than to enjoy his work, because that is his lot. For who can bring him to see what will happen after him?

Ecclesiastes 4

Oppression, toil, friendlessness

¹ Again I looked and saw all the oppression that was taking place under the sun:

> I saw the tears of the oppressed –
> and they have no comforter;
> power was on the side of their oppressors –
> and they have no comforter.

² And I declared that the dead,
> who had already died,
> are happier than the living,
> who are still alive.

³ But better than both
> is he who has not yet been,
> who has not seen the evil
> that is done under the sun.

⁴ And I saw that all labour and all achievement spring from man's envy of his neighbour. This too is meaningless, a chasing after the wind.

⁵ The fool folds his hands
   and ruins himself.
⁶ Better one handful with tranquillity
   than two handfuls with toil
   and chasing after the wind.

⁷ Again I saw something meaningless under the sun:

⁸ There was a man all alone;
   he had neither son nor brother.
   There was no end to his toil,
   yet his eyes were not content with his wealth.
   '"For whom am I toiling," he asked,' and why am I
   depriving myself of enjoyment?'
   This too is meaningless –
   a miserable business!

⁹ Two are better than one,
   because they have a good return for their work:
¹⁰ If one falls down,
   his friend can help him up.
   But pity the man who falls
   and has no one to help him up!
¹¹ Also, if two lie down together, they will keep warm.
   But how can one keep warm alone?
¹² Though one may be overpowered,
   two can defend themselves.
   A cord of three strands is not quickly broken.

Advancement is meaningless

¹³ Better a poor but wise youth than an old but foolish king
   who no longer knows how to take warning. ¹⁴ The youth
   may have come from prison to the kingship, or he may
   have been born in poverty within his kingdom. ¹⁵ I saw
   that all who lived and walked under the sun followed
   the youth, the king's successor. ¹⁶ There was no end to all
   the people who were before them. But those who came
   later were not pleased with the successor. This too is
   meaningless, a chasing after the wind.

Ecclesiastes 5

Stand in awe of God

¹ Guard your steps when you go to the house of God. Go near to listen rather than to offer the sacrifice of fools, who do not know that they do wrong.

² Do not be quick with your mouth,
do not be hasty in your heart
to utter anything before God.
God is in heaven
and you are on earth,
so let your words be few.
³ As a dream comes when there are many cares,
so the speech of a fool when there are many words.
⁴ When you make a vow to God, do not delay in fulfilling it.
He has no pleasure in fools; fulfil your vow. ⁵ It is
better not to vow than to make a vow and not fulfil it.
⁶ Do not let your mouth lead you into sin. And do not
protest to the temple messenger, 'My vow was a
mistake.' Why should God be angry at what you say
and destroy the work of your hands? ⁷ Much dreaming
and many words are meaningless. Therefore stand in
awe of God.

Riches are meaningless

⁸ If you see the poor oppressed in a district, and justice and rights denied, do not be surprised at such things; for one official is eyed by a higher one, and over them both are others higher still. ⁹ The increase from the land is taken by all; the king himself profits from the fields.

¹⁰ Whoever loves money never has money enough;
whoever loves wealth is never satisfied with his income.
This too is meaningless.

¹¹ As goods increase,
so do those who consume them.
And what benefit are they to the owner
except to feast his eyes on them?

¹² The sleep of a labourer is sweet,
  whether he eats little or much,
  but the abundance of a rich man
  permits him no sleep.

¹³ I have seen a grievous evil under the sun:
  wealth hoarded to the harm of its owner,
¹⁴ or wealth lost through some misfortune,
  so that when he has a son
  there is nothing left for him.
¹⁵ Naked a man comes from his mother's womb,
  and as he comes, so he departs.
  He takes nothing from his labour
  that he can carry in his hand.

¹⁶ This too is a grievous evil:

  As a man comes, so he departs,
  and what does he gain,
  since he toils for the wind?
¹⁷ All his days he eats in darkness,
  with great frustration, affliction and anger.

¹⁸ Then I realised that it is good and proper for a man to eat and drink, and to find satisfaction in his toilsome labour under the sun during the few days of life God has given him – for this is his lot. ¹⁹ Moreover, when God gives any man wealth and possessions, and enables him to enjoy them, to accept his lot and be happy in his work – this is a gift of God. ²⁰ He seldom reflects on the days of his life, because God keeps him occupied with gladness of heart.

Ecclesiastes 6

¹ I have seen another evil under the sun, and it weighs heavily on men: ² God gives a man wealth, possessions and honour, so that he lacks nothing his heart desires, but God does not enable him to enjoy them, and a stranger enjoys them instead. This is meaningless, a grievous evil.
³ A man may have a hundred children and live many years; yet no matter how long he lives, if he cannot enjoy his prosperity and does not receive proper burial, I say that

a stillborn child is better off than he. [4] It comes without meaning, it departs in darkness, and in darkness its name is shrouded. [5] Though it never saw the sun or knew anything, it has more rest than does that man – [6] even if he lives a thousand years twice over but fails to enjoy his prosperity. Do not all go to the same place?

[7] All man's efforts are for his mouth,
   yet his appetite is never satisfied.
[8] What advantage has a wise man over a fool?
   What does a poor man gain
   by knowing how to conduct himself before others?
[9] Better what the eye sees
   than the roving of the appetite.
   This too is meaningless,
   a chasing after the wind.
[10] Whatever exists has already been named,
   and what man is has been known;
   no man can contend
   with one who is stronger than he.
[11] The more the words,
   the less the meaning,
   and how does that profit anyone?

[12] For who knows what is good for a man in life, during the few and meaningless days he passes through like a shadow? Who can tell him what will happen under the sun after he is gone?

Ecclesiastes 7

Wisdom

[1] A good name is better than fine perfume,
   and the day of death better than the day of birth.
[2] It is better to go to a house of mourning
   than to go to a house of feasting,
   for death is the destiny of every man;
   the living should take this to heart.

³ Sorrow is better than laughter,
  because a sad face is good for the heart.
⁴ The heart of the wise is in the house of mourning,
  but the heart of fools is in the house of pleasure.
⁵ It is better to heed a wise man's rebuke
  than to listen to the song of fools.
⁶ Like the crackling of thorns under the pot,
  so is the laughter of fools.
  This too is meaningless.

⁷ Extortion turns a wise man into a fool,
  and a bribe corrupts the heart.

⁸ The end of a matter is better than its beginning,
  and patience is better than pride.
⁹ Do not be quickly provoked in your spirit,
  for anger resides in the lap of fools.

¹⁰ Do not say, 'Why were the old days better than these?'
   For it is not wise to ask such questions.

¹¹ Wisdom, like an inheritance, is a good thing
   and benefits those who see the sun.
¹² Wisdom is a shelter
   as money is a shelter,
   but the advantage of knowledge is this:
   that wisdom preserves the life of its possessor.

¹³ Consider what God has done:

   Who can straighten
   what he has made crooked?
¹⁴ When times are good, be happy;
   but when times are bad, consider:
   God has made the one
   as well as the other.
   Therefore, a man cannot discover
   anything about his future.

¹⁵ In this meaningless life of mine I have seen both of these:
   a righteous man perishing in his righteousness,
   and a wicked man living long in his wickedness.

16 Do not be over-righteous,
  neither be overwise –
  why destroy yourself?
17 Do not be overwicked,
  and do not be a fool –
  why die before your time?
18 It is good to grasp the one
  and not let go of the other.
  The man who fears God will avoid all extremes.

19 Wisdom makes one wise man more powerful
  than ten rulers in a city.

20 There is not a righteous man on earth
  who does what is right and never sins.
21 Do not pay attention to every word people say,
  or you may hear your servant cursing you –
22 for you know in your heart
  that many times you yourself have cursed others.

23 All this I tested by wisdom and I said,

  'I am determined to be wise' –
  but this was beyond me.
24 Whatever wisdom may be,
  it is far off and most profound –
  who can discover it?
25 So I turned my mind to understand,
  to investigate and to search out wisdom and the scheme of
  things
  and to understand the stupidity of wickedness
  and the madness of folly.

26 I find more bitter than death
  the woman who is a snare,
  whose heart is a trap
  and whose hands are chains.
  The man who pleases God will escape her,
  but the sinner she will ensnare.

27 'Look,' says the Teacher, 'this is what I have
  discovered:

'Adding one thing to another to discover the scheme of
things –
²⁸ while I was still searching
but not finding –
I found one upright man among a thousand,
but not one upright woman among them all.
²⁹ This only have I found:
God made mankind upright,
but men have gone in search of many schemes.'

Ecclesiastes 8

¹ Who is like the wise man?
Who knows the explanation of things?
Wisdom brightens a man's face
and changes its hard appearance.

Obey the king

² Obey the king's command, I say, because you took an
oath before God. ³ Do not be in a hurry to leave the king's
presence. Do not stand up for a bad cause, for he will do
whatever he pleases. ⁴ Since a king's word is supreme, who
can say to him, 'What are you doing?'

⁵ Whoever obeys his command will come to no harm,
and the wise heart will know the proper time and
procedure.
⁶ For there is a proper time and procedure for every matter,
though a man's misery weighs heavily upon him.

⁷ Since no man knows the future,
who can tell him what is to come?
⁸ No man has power over the wind to contain it;
so no one has power over the day of his death.
As no one is discharged in time of war,
so wickedness will not release those who practise it.

⁹ All this I saw, as I applied my mind to everything done
under the sun. There is a time when a man lords it over

others to his own hurt. [10] Then too, I saw the wicked buried
– those who used to come and go from the holy place and
receive praise in the city where they did this. This too is
meaningless. [11] When the sentence for a crime is not quickly
carried out, the hearts of the people are filled with schemes
to do wrong. [12] Although a wicked man commits a hundred
crimes and still lives a long time, I know that it will go
better with God-fearing men, who are reverent before
God. [13] Yet because the wicked do not fear God, it will not
go well with them, and their days will not lengthen like a
shadow.

[14] There is something else meaningless that occurs on earth:
righteous men who get what the wicked deserve, and
wicked men who get what the righteous deserve. This too,
I say, is meaningless. [15] So I commend the enjoyment of life,
because nothing is better for a man under the sun than to
eat and drink and be glad. Then joy will accompany him in
his work all the days of the life God has given him under
the sun.

[16] When I applied my mind to know wisdom and to observe
man's labour on earth – his eyes not seeing sleep day or
night – [17] then I saw all that God has done. No one can
comprehend what goes on under the sun. Despite all his
efforts to search it out, man cannot discover its meaning.
Even if a wise man claims he knows, he cannot really
comprehend it.

Ecclesiastes 9

A common destiny for all

[1] So I reflected on all this and concluded that the righteous
and the wise and what they do are in God's hands, but no
man knows whether love or hate awaits him. [2] All share a
common destiny – the righteous and the wicked, the good
and the bad, the clean and the unclean, those who offer
sacrifices and those who do not.

As it is with the good man,
so with the sinner;

as it is with those who take oaths,
so with those who are afraid to take them.

[3] This is the evil in everything that happens under the
sun: The same destiny overtakes all. The hearts of men,
moreover, are full of evil and there is madness in their
hearts while they live, and afterward they join the dead.
[4] Anyone who is among the living has hope – even a live
dog is better off than a dead lion!

[5] For the living know that they will die,
but the dead know nothing;
they have no further reward,
and even the memory of them is forgotten.
[6] Their love, their hate
and their jealousy have long since vanished;
never again will they have a part
in anything that happens under the sun.

[7] Go, eat your food with gladness, and drink your wine
with a joyful heart, for it is now that God favours what
you do. [8] Always be clothed in white, and always anoint
your head with oil. [9] Enjoy life with your wife, whom you
love, all the days of this meaningless life that God has
given you under the sun – all your meaningless days. For
this is your lot in life and in your toilsome labour under
the sun. [10] Whatever your hand finds to do, do it with
all your might, for in the grave, where you are going,
there is neither working nor planning nor knowledge nor
wisdom.

[11] I have seen something else under the sun:

The race is not to the swift
or the battle to the strong,
nor does food come to the wise
or wealth to the brilliant
or favour to the learned;
but time and chance happen to them all.

[12] Moreover, no man knows when his hour will come:

As fish are caught in a cruel net,
or birds are taken in a snare,
so men are trapped by evil times
that fall unexpectedly upon them.

Wisdom better than folly

¹³ I also saw under the sun this example of wisdom that greatly impressed me: ¹⁴ There was once a small city with only a few people in it. And a powerful king came against it, surrounded it and built huge siege works against it. ¹⁵ Now there lived in that city a man poor but wise, and he saved the city by his wisdom. But nobody remembered that poor man. ¹⁶ So I said, 'Wisdom is better than strength.' But the poor man's wisdom is despised, and his words are no longer heeded.

¹⁷ The quiet words of the wise are more to be heeded
than the shouts of a ruler of fools.
¹⁸ Wisdom is better than weapons of war,
but one sinner destroys much good.

Ecclesiastes 10

¹ As dead flies give perfume a bad smell,
so a little folly outweighs wisdom and honour.
² The heart of the wise inclines to the right,
but the heart of the fool to the left.
³ Even as he walks along the road,
the fool lacks sense
and shows everyone how stupid he is.
⁴ If a ruler's anger rises against you,
do not leave your post;
calmness can lay great errors to rest.

⁵ There is an evil I have seen under the sun,
the sort of error that arises from a ruler:
⁶ Fools are put in many high positions,
while the rich occupy the low ones.

⁷ I have seen slaves on horseback,
while princes go on foot like slaves.

⁸ Whoever digs a pit may fall into it;
whoever breaks through a wall may be bitten by a snake.
⁹ Whoever quarries stones may be injured by them;
whoever splits logs may be endangered by them.

¹⁰ If the axe is dull
and its edge unsharpened,
more strength is needed
but skill will bring success.

¹¹ If a snake bites before it is charmed,
there is no profit for the charmer.

¹² Words from a wise man's mouth are gracious,
but a fool is consumed by his own lips.
¹³ At the beginning his words are folly;
at the end they are wicked madness –
¹⁴ and the fool multiplies words.

No one knows what is coming –
who can tell him what will happen after him?

¹⁵ A fool's work wearies him;
he does not know the way to town.

¹⁶ Woe to you, O land whose king was a servant
and whose princes feast in the morning.
¹⁷ Blessed are you, O land whose king is of noble birth
and whose princes eat at a proper time –
for strength and not for drunkenness.

¹⁸ If a man is lazy, the rafters sag;
if his hands are idle, the house leaks.

¹⁹ A feast is made for laughter,
and wine makes life merry,
but money is the answer for everything.

20 Do not revile the king even in your thoughts,
   or curse the rich in your bedroom,
   because a bird of the air may carry your words,
   and a bird on the wing may report what you say.

Ecclesiastes 11

Bread upon the waters

1 Cast your bread upon the waters,
   for after many days you will find it again.
2 Give portions to seven, yes to eight,
   for you do not know what disaster may come upon the
   land.

3 If clouds are full of water,
   they pour rain upon the earth.
   Whether a tree falls to the south or to the north,
   in the place where it falls, there will it lie.
4 Whoever watches the wind will not plant;
   whoever looks at the clouds will not reap.

5 As you do not know the path of the wind,
   or how the body is formed in a mother's womb,
   so you cannot understand the work of God,
   the Maker of all things.

6 Sow your seed in the morning,
   and at evening let not your hands be idle,
   for you do not know which will succeed,
   whether this or that,
   or whether both will do equally well.

Remember your creator while young

7 Light is sweet,
   and it pleases the eyes to see the sun.
8 However many years a man may live,
   let him enjoy them all.
   But let him remember the days of darkness,
   for they will be many.
   Everything to come is meaningless.

9 Be happy, young man, while you are young,
and let your heart give you joy in the days of your youth.
Follow the ways of your heart
and whatever your eyes see,
but know that for all these things
God will bring you to judgement.
10 So then, banish anxiety from your heart
and cast off the troubles of your body,
for youth and vigour are meaningless.

Ecclesiastes 12

1 Remember your Creator
in the days of your youth,
before the days of trouble come
and the years approach when you will say,
'I find no pleasure in them' –
2 before the sun and the light
and the moon and the stars grow dark,
and the clouds return after the rain;
3 when the keepers of the house tremble,
and the strong men stoop,
when the grinders cease because they are few,
and those looking through the windows grow dim;
4 when the doors to the street are closed
and the sound of grinding fades;
when men rise up at the sound of birds,
but all their songs grow faint;
5 when men are afraid of heights
and of dangers in the streets;
when the almond tree blossoms
and the grasshopper drags himself along
and desire no longer is stirred.
Then man goes to his eternal home
and mourners go about the streets.

6 Remember him – before the silver cord is severed,
or the golden bowl is broken;
before the pitcher is shattered at the spring,
or the wheel broken at the well,

⁷ and the dust returns to the ground it came from,
and the spirit returns to God who gave it.

⁸ 'Meaningless! Meaningless!' says the Teacher.
'Everything is meaningless!'

The conclusion of the matter

⁹ Not only was the Teacher wise, but also he imparted
knowledge to the people. He pondered and searched out
and set in order many proverbs. ¹⁰ The Teacher searched to
find just the right words, and what he wrote was upright
and true.
¹¹ The words of the wise are like goads, their collected sayings
like firmly embedded nails – given by one Shepherd. ¹² Be
warned, my son, of anything in addition to them.
Of making many books there is no end, and much study
wearies the body.

¹³ Now all has been heard;
here is the conclusion of the matter:
Fear God and keep his commandments,
for this is the whole duty of man.
¹⁴ For God will bring every deed into judgement,
including every hidden thing,
whether it is good or evil.